The
Gifts
of
Change

Nancy Christie

ATRIA PAPERBACK
New York London Toronto Sydney

BEYOND WORDS
Hillsboro, Oregon

ATRIA PAPERBACK
A Division of Simon & Schuster, Inc.
1230 Avenue of the Americas
New York, NY 10020

BEYOND WORDS
Beyond Words Publishing, Inc.
20827 N.W. Cornell Road, Suite 500
Hillsboro, Oregon 97124-9808
503-531-8700

Editor: Julie Steigerwaldt
Managing editor: Sarabeth Blakey
Proofreader: Jade Chan
Cover design: Jerry Soga
Composition: William H. Brunson Typography Services

ATRIA PAPERBACK and colophon are trademarks of Simon & Schuster, Inc. Beyond Words Publishing is a division of Simon & Schuster, Inc.

Printed in the United States of America

Library of Congress Cataloging-in-Publication Data

Christie, Nancy, 1954–
    The gifts of change / Nancy Christie.
        p. cm.
    ISBN 1-58270-119-9 (pbk.)
    1. Women—Conduct of life.   2. Change (Psychology)   I. Title.
BJ1610.C54   2004
155.2'4—dc22

                                                    2004006799

The corporate mission of Beyond Words Publishing, Inc.: *Inspire to Integrity*

To my parents, Joseph and Mary Ress,
with all my love and gratitude.

Part III. Moving Forward

Contents

Acknowledgements

So many people have helped me bring this book to fruition, for which I owe them much gratitude and appreciation:

My publisher—Cynthia Black and the wonderful and supportive staff at Beyond Words Publishing: editors Beth Caldwell Hoyt, Sarabeth Blakey, Julie Steigerwaldt, and Jade Chan. Their belief in the book and in me, and their invaluable assistance, insight, dedication, and creativity have made *The Gifts of Change* more than what I had expected or hoped for.

My contributors—who opened their hearts and lives to me, making the book so much richer and more meaningful.

My friends—who have shared so many changes with me and allowed me to include their stories in this book. A special and heartfelt thanks to Itala Landers, who has been part of my life for more than twenty years and believed in me even when I doubted myself.

My literary support network—all the wonderful authors whose words have inspired me: Sue Patton Thoele, Rena Pederson, Carol Keeffe, Carolyn Heilbrun, Tillie Olsen, Joan Borysenko, Thomas Crum, and so many others. A special thanks to Mark Helprin, who took the time to encourage a self-doubting writer, and Susan Jeffers, who was with me in spirit as I entered the realm of self-employment.

My family—my parents, Joe and Mary Ress, whose support was a rod that kept me upright when I faltered. My children, Samantha and Joe, and my grandson Zachary, who were not only the catalyst for so many changes that occurred in my life but the source of strength that enabled me to grow from them. And to all the readers who are part of my Community of Change, bon voyage as you journey toward your goals!

Introduction

As a child I envisioned life as a succession of identical moments, strung like beads on a cord of stability. The only change would come at predicted intervals: seasons would arrive and depart, holidays would be celebrated and then forgotten, and life would continue with a degree of reliability that was as unquestioned as it was consistent.

Little did I realize that adulthood would be fraught with change—transition upon transition and minor and major alterations to my life's landscape. Over the years every aspect of my life has been in flux at one time or another as I have struggled to adapt to a myriad of alterations, both professional and personal.

Some of the changes were welcome, chosen, and even sought after. Others were not so desired and brought with them elements of pain, disappointment, heartache, and sorrow. But all were transforming experiences, especially when I stopped battling the changes and started welcoming them.

I realized that without change there can be no growth. The key is to not spend energy avoiding change but to embrace it willingly, using each experience to develop new strengths and abilities to prepare for the next series of transformations. It's not about blind acceptance but rather actively searching for the positive aspects in all our life experiences. And while we may be able to point to major events as life changing, sometimes it is the inconspicuous times that can help us develop a new perspective on our lives. This is the gift that comes with change.

When we welcome change, we find opportunities for growth and development and new strengths and hidden abilities become apparent to us. Embracing the changes that come into our lives allows us to learn from them and to ultimately create a richer, deeper, more fulfilling life.

My hope is that the pages ahead will inspire you to look closer at how you deal with the inevitability of change, reevaluate your goals, and embrace the opportunities for growth that are right before you. Open your eyes. Open your mind. Open your heart. Embrace the gifts of change.

Part I:
Inviting Change

1

Weaving Our Tapestry

Have you ever watched someone creating a tapestry? Different colors of thread are used, and it is up to the weaver to know when and where each hue should be brought from the back to take its rightful place in the pattern. But even with all its colors, a well-designed tapestry has one major shade. We speak of a piece as having blue tones or a red influence. There may be areas where that color is almost nonexistent, but it is always present in the piece as a whole.

In our life tapestry we have many threads that represent various parts of our life. We are wife, mother, daughter, sister, employee, church member, and friend, but our primary color is the thread that connects us to our own existence, the one that links us to the deepest part of ourselves and our driving force. If we lose that thread, its absence will be noticed—perhaps not right away, perhaps not until the other threads are woven out of the pattern, as our children grow into adulthood, our friends move away, our parents die, and our spouse follows his or her own thread. But eventually we will realize that our tapestry has lost its unifying color and its heart.

How can we identify our primary color and keep it woven firmly in place? Our color should bring us joy—not happiness, which is transitory, but true joy. We are happy when we don't owe more income tax, happy when the scale registers a five-pound weight loss, happy when we get a raise at work. True joy goes beyond happiness. It's a feeling of rightness, a sense of fitness and purpose, a feeling that has an almost spiritual dimension to it.

Joy is what the artist feels as she puts the finishing touches on the canvas, knowing that she has integrated her thoughts and emotions into a unified piece. Joy is what a mother feels when she holds her newborn for the first time and recognizes her place in the scheme of life. Joy comes from knowing that we are an essential part of something greater, that we are fulfilling our role in life, and that while there are many things that we *can* and *will* do, there are some that we *must* do. Joy comes from recognizing our unique abilities and using them to their fullest extent.

Motivational author Josh Hinds reminded us, "Whether or not we realize it, each of us has a special gift inside us just waiting to surface! . . . The important thing here is not what your gift is as much as that you develop it so that you can share it with those around you and in the process further your own personal life!"[1]

It may take some investigation to find out what your primary color is, when so many colors are woven into your life. For my part, I am a wife, a mother of grown children, a grandmother, a daughter, a sister, and a friend. I have owned businesses and I have been an employee. To varying degrees, each responsibility has brought me a certain measure of satisfaction and, even at times, joy. But my primary source of fulfillment doesn't originate from any of those positions. I am, first and foremost, a writer. For me, that is the one thread of continuity that has been woven through my existence since I first learned to form letters.

There were times in my life when my writing all but disappeared, when the closest I came to creativity was concocting recipes or jotting down a grocery list. But writing has always been the one aspect of my existence independent of anything else in my life. My most joyful, fulfilled moments come when my writing is going well, and my times of despair are never greater than when I can't express my thoughts and emotions on paper. When I am writing and sharing my thoughts, feelings, and ideas with the world, I know in the very core of my being that I am doing what I was put here to do.

My sister-in-law Shirley finds her joy in God. And given the fact that for most of her adult life she has suffered from severe health problems, it is all the more admirable that her faith has not been shaken but instead strengthened. She takes her joy and expresses it outwardly, doing volunteer work for her church and the community at large and being a wellspring of love for her family. By following her own thread, she has woven a pattern filled with positive energy instead of negativity and resentment for her physical condition.

My friend Dianne is a beautiful woman who is married to a loving man, is financially secure, and has healthy children and grandchildren. One would believe that she doesn't need to look for her joy, but she found her purpose in life through her work with domestic violence victims. By incorporating this thread into her life's pattern, she has helped many others mend the tears in their fabric.

We cannot keep our thread of joy within the pattern we weave unless we first take the time to identify it. To find your primary thread, ask yourself the following questions: If I were removed from my current existence or if my friends and family members ceased to exist, what would I be left with? What essential part of my being would still be with me?

In *Believing in Ourselves: The Journey Ahead* by Arlene F. Benedict, American author Charlotte Perkins Gilman reminded us that "the first duty of a human being is to find your real job and do it."[2] This "real job" should not be determined by its income potential; just because it doesn't bring in money doesn't rob it of its value. A painter may never sell one picture or may even lose money from paints and canvas, and yet he or she derives a great sense of rightness from the time spent engaged in creating pieces of art. A volunteer may spend hours making a difference in her own little corner of the world and never receive acknowledgement or compensation. But the satisfaction she receives—and the benefits others reap—far outweigh the energy she expends. While books like Marsha Sinetar's *Do What You Love, the Money Will Follow* point out that it is possible to be psychically and financially rewarded within your occupation, it may not happen right away or even at all. And it shouldn't matter. Your primary thread's worth doesn't lie in its market value but in its intrinsic benefit to your life.

Sometimes as we explore our joy, we dissuade ourselves from what seems right, believing that a true primary thread is one that we already have a proven aptitude for. It can't be art, we reason, because we don't know anything about perspective or technique. So we put the brush down, turn the canvas to the wall, and go back to more familiar tasks. But in doing so, we have lost the opportunity to discover hidden talents. We have an obligation—a sacred duty—to ourselves to explore all our abilities, even those we didn't know we had.

You may find that as you define your joy, you must also deal with conflicts that arise with others in your life. For example, if a woman decides that her primary thread lies in the medical profession and plans to go to school, knowing that this is the right decision for her, the rest of her family may only see that she will no longer have the time and energy to devote to them as she had in the past. They might feel abandoned, threatened, and resentful, and she may wonder if she is being selfish to follow her thread, since it disturbs the patterns of others. She can decide to go ahead with her plans while working with her family to make the transition as easy as possible, or she might postpone her plans, until the need for her at home is not as great. Or she may tell her family that it is her turn to pursue her goal and that they will have to adapt.

The key is that her decision—and yours—must be made in peace, not in anger, nor with a sense of sacrifice or resentment. Negative emotions lead to negative outcomes, and if your decision is colored with harmful emotions, that sought-after primary thread will become a noose around your neck.

Discovering your thread of joy can be a lifelong process. Not everyone is born with a clearly defined sense of purpose.

For some, it comes after a series of life lessons has stripped away all the nonessential aspects of life. But once found, this thread is what we hold on to when it seems that there is nothing else left. It defines us, differentiates us from other people, guides us throughout our life, and keeps us on the right path. When we find our own thread of joy, the rewards will far outweigh the work as the pattern we are creating finally has its true heart.

2

Exploring Our Possibilities

I remember watching my daughter, Samantha, when she discovered her hands. She turned those fat palms toward herself and then away, raised her arms a bit and let them fall. The look on her face was a mix of concentration and awe. She seemed truly amazed that those chubby hands were there and that she, by simply thinking movement, could raise them. There was no awareness yet of the hands being hers. They were just hands and she was seeing them clearly for the very first time.

Everything infants do is for the first time. There is no past experience to draw on, no preconceived notion of an object's purpose. A spoon can just as easily be a source of noise as well as a carrier of nourishment. A dog can be a playmate or a pillow. There is no right or wrong use of an object, no correct or incorrect behavior. That comes later, along with the word "no," the act of toilet training, and the endless progression of conventions and dictates that turns babies into productive members of society.

For the most part, these series of rules and regulations are essential elements of growing up. Without them, we would be a society of anarchists or, at the very least, incredibly selfish people. But as we learn how to behave and what constitutes acceptable use of objects, we lose our sense of imagination and wonder and place limits on possibilities.

A two-year-old sees a blanket as a comfort object, a six-year-old as a tent, an adult as a bed covering. Adults establish definitions for everything in life and then refuse to explore alternatives. No synonyms are acceptable; there is but one word and that is the only word we use.

But this thinking is narrow and limiting. By not exploring other possibilities, we rob ourselves of life's richness and gradually erode our sense of creativity. We must "keep writing talents strong and sharp, nourish the space where they came from ... see fine art, hear soothing music, taste wonderful foods, touch fantastic texture or smell exotic aromas,"[1] said poet Joyce Locking.

This advice even applies to those who do not write. Every time we see examples of another's creativity, we should be encouraged to explore our own. Every time the world comes into view (which is daily, if we have our eyes open) we should make an effort to really look at it. A scarlet cardinal is not just a bird, a delicate narcissus is not just a flower, and the evening sky aflame with red and orange is not just a signal that night approaches. They are all causes for wonderment, appreciation, and gratitude that we are here to witness.

But it's difficult to really see, to pay attention to the actual world, when we are too busy with the world in our mind. We are in such a rush to move on to the next thought that we perceive, identify, and dismiss almost in the same instant. We miss so much of what is really there because our vision never goes past the surface.

One day my grandson taught me the art of exploring possibilities. Samantha, sick with the flu on New Year's Day, asked me to take the baby for a few hours so she could get some sleep. And while we were out, would I mind picking up her prescription for her? Like a good mom/grandma, I agreed, finding myself within the hour in a busy drugstore with Zachary, who was not quite a year old and full of energy.

Faced with a thirty-minute wait for the prescription to be filled, I decided to stay in the store, easier, I thought, than dealing with a squirming baby and the intricacies of a car seat harness. So Zachary and I traversed the aisles, and since I was forced keep all my attention on him, I was inadvertently drawn into his world.

Through his eyes, I saw not bottles of shampoos and conditioners but a rainbow of colors. The display of bows, ribbons, and wrapping paper became a series of finger-tempting textures, while the perfume aisle enveloped my nose with indescribable fragrances.

"Look, Zack," I said as I dangled a bright red dog leash in front of him, snapping and unsnapping the hook to his great delight. "Here, Zack," I exclaimed and tossed a bag of cotton balls at him, just to hear him giggle.

Had I been alone, I would have been tapping my foot, impatiently glancing at my watch, and fuming that my precious time was being spent waiting in line. But the baby's presence forced me to see where I was instead of being frustrated over where I wasn't. Zack gave me the unexpected delight of recapturing the wonder in everyday things.

That experience encouraged me to make some changes in my life. I started with the birdfeeding regimen.

On a tree outside my office window, I had hung two finch feeders, two regular bird feeders, and a suet cake holder, yet I rarely looked up from my computer screen to see what new avian visitors had found the thistle, sunflower seed, and cracked corn. But after that day with Zack, I bought a small notebook and a bird identification guide. Now several times each morning, I take a much-needed break from my work to look outside and see who has come to the bird buffet. I check my visitors' colors, wing and tail shape, body size, and call, and then consult my book to find out if it is a house sparrow or a wren, a junco or a titmouse before carefully noting the birds on a dated page. Each morning, I am drawn into their world and, by extension, the entire environment. My own world has been enlarged because I have stopped to see instead of rushing on to the next task. Checking on the bird feeder isn't a task to complete on my to-do list but an opportunity to clear my mind, learn about another species, and connect with nature.

It is not impossible to raise our level of awareness and begin exploring possibilities; it just takes some effort. By recapturing a sense of imagination and wonder, we dazzle our senses and enrich our lives. Albert Einstein noted, "There are only two ways to live your life. One is as though nothing is a miracle. The other is as though everything is a miracle."[2] Given the choice, a miraculous view of life seems preferable.

But we shouldn't stop at the outside environment as we are sharpening our sense of awareness. We also need to turn our eyes inward, take a fresh look at our internal landscape, and explore all our abilities; otherwise we rob ourselves of possibilities. If we shape our life to follow only one path, we will never explore the hidden byways that may lead to a more fulfilled existence.

This doesn't mean that the secretary has to give up a paid job to explore a career in the theater, nor should the doctor trade a stethoscope for an artist's brush. It simply means that by finding out all that we are capable of being and all the traits, abilities, and gifts that we possess, we will be able to lead a more fulfilled and enriched life. Inner growth leads to a greater sense of personal achievement that then influences our external existence. "Human beings, by changing the inner attitudes of their minds, can change the outer aspects of their lives,"³ said American psychologist and philosopher William James.

Take a moment now and number the lines on a sheet of paper from one to ten. Without taking the time to pause and reflect, write down your identities. Parent, daughter, nurse, insurance agent—note them all. Below this list, number from one to ten again and write down all your abilities or those you want to explore—even if you haven't yet explored them to any great length.

How well do the two lists match up? Do the roles on the first list use just a fraction of those traits detailed on the second? Do you have abilities that are being underutilized or even totally ignored? Have you limited yourself to only a few select identities rather than allowing other roles and abilities to be incorporated into your life?

Now, from one to ten, list your dreams—those personal mountains you want to climb, those deep waters you want to dive into. What do you want to be? Who do you want to be? If you had only one year to live, how would you spend it? If money and time weren't obstacles, what would you be doing with your life?

Are you finding it difficult to write the third list? Is your inner censor monitoring your thoughts, telling you how foolish, impractical, or selfish your dreams are? Close your ears and write your dreams and desires anyway. This makes them real and gives them life and a chance to come true.

Now look at your three lists. The first represents the world you have created; the second, all your abilities, tapped and untapped. If you are very lucky, the third list will have some connection with the first and second ones. But if each list is separate and unrelated to the others, you have so much more potential waiting to be explored.

Take these lists and begin now to integrate the person you want to be into the life you are living now. Choose one attribute that has been hiding, bring it to the forefront, and use it to take baby steps toward one of your dreams. You may find that it is closer to becoming reality than you had imagined.

For instance, are you a parent with a talent for drawing who dreams of becoming an artist? Create a picture book for your child, filled with illustrations of your life together. Do you want to make a difference in your community but need the income from your current job? Volunteer your time and talents at a local charity. By bringing some element of your dream into your current existence, you are opening the door to making it a reality.

We must explore our inner world the way we would explore a foreign country. We need to throw away all our preconceived ideas, limiting beliefs, and restricting roles. We have spent a lifetime with ourselves, but do we know who we really are? To what extent has our identity been shaped by others or our perception restricted by events or circumstances?

Sometimes we refuse to look at ourselves because we are afraid of what we might see. Sometimes we resist searching within for fear that what we find may upset the life that we have so carefully created. When we find out who we are and all that we are capable of becoming, we may also find that we are outgrowing the confines of our current existence. But it is only through self-exploration that we can find out who we really are and what more we can do with our lives. If knowledge is power, then self-knowledge is the greatest power of all, for it affords us the ability to create a new reality that encompasses all that we are and all that we can be.

3

Betsy's Boots

My girlfriend Betsy once gave me a pair of brown suede boots with a braid across the instep and silver trim on the heels and toes. My first thought was "These aren't 'me.' They are too pointed, have too high of a heel, and are too fashionable. These aren't the kind of boots I would buy at all."

And then I slipped them on. The boots fit like they were made for my feet. The little bit of a heel (not that high after all) added two inches to my five-foot-two frame and immediately gave me a different perspective on the world. Suede was not something I would have bought for myself because it would have been too expensive and too frivolous, but wearing it made me feel different, as though I were suddenly more stylish, more fashionable, and worth every cent.

Now I wear the boots every chance I get, and I notice that I walk a little more boldly, stand a little more assertively, and feel more daring when I do. If the clothes make the man, then the boots, in this case, make the woman.

I started to think about how many times I have turned down clothes, makeup, or accessories because they weren't "me." How many times have I rejected seeing a movie because I was certain I wouldn't like it, or refrained from trying a certain food because it was too unusual to me? Worse yet, how many opportunities have I passed up because they didn't seem right or safe to try, because they weren't "my kind of thing"?

If I could be so wrong about something as simple as a pair of boots, how well did I really know myself? Had I simply accepted a very one-dimensional view of myself, refusing to try something different because I was convinced in advance that it wouldn't fit?

Somewhere along the line I had decided who I was and who I couldn't be. I hadn't left room for growth or change and had become locked into a certain identity: a fortysomething woman with two kids and a grandchild. Did that mean that I couldn't be something more or even someone else?

Most of us fall victim to confinement sooner or later. We struggle so hard and for so long to figure out who we are that when we get an answer, we want to stop looking and stop growing. There is comfort in waking up each morning and knowing who you are, what is expected of you, and the level of success you can reasonably hope to attain. After all, adulthood is fraught with uncertainty. Once we can settle into a groove, it is so much easier to reject new challenges.

But as comfortable and stable as that base of operations may be, it can also become very stultifying and restricting. We never challenge ourselves or our concept of our abilities. We never explore those other dimensions that make up who we are and never excavate through layers of habit to find gems hidden below the surface. We opt for security, forgetting that the only true security lies within faith in our own abilities.

To test how stuck you are, try to do one thing different, one action you would deem out of character. It needn't be anything too extreme—just something that you would ordinarily reject out of hand. Does that prospect seem a little silly, wasteful, or maybe even a little frightening? Good. Do it anyway.

Challenge your body. Take a weight-training class, go for a ten-mile hike, or try ballroom dancing or rock-climbing. Challenge your mind. Learn a new language, play Scrabble or chess against a really good opponent, or attend a foreign film. Challenge your heart. Volunteer at a nursing home, collect donations for a worthy cause, or have a heart-to-heart talk with someone you haven't gotten along with.

Whatever you try should be a little difficult, a little challenging, a bit of a stretch, and wholly without expectations or judgment. This isn't about succeeding or failing. Just making the attempt qualifies it as a success, even if the heaviest weight you can lift is three pounds, the biggest words you can come up with in Scrabble are four letters long, or the amount of donations you collect amounts to less than fifty dollars. It's the attempt that matters. Each time you try, you gain more strength and confidence, making the next endeavor more possible. Mihaly Csikszentmihalyi said it best in *Creativity: Flow and the Psychology of Discovery and Invention*: "Even without success, creative persons find joy in a job well done. Learning for its own sake is rewarding."[1]

To avoid being typecast, actors take on roles that will stretch their abilities and develop their skills. When she is in character, Meryl Streep is no longer a New Jersey native but instead a completely believable Holocaust victim, a Danish coffee plantation owner in Africa, or a mother surrendering her child to her ex-husband. Writers explore different genres, relying on pseudonyms to create different literary identities. When she wrote historical novels, mystery writer Agatha Christie used the name Mary Westmacott. Feminist scholar Carolyn Heilbrun did double duty as best-selling mystery writer Amanda Cross. We, too, have more than one name and one identity. Each time our life changes because of marriage, parenthood, divorce, or job transition, we gain a new title and, with it, the opportunity to expand our repertoire.

Once I started wearing the boots, I stopped thinking of myself as the person I knew and began wondering what else I could do and who else I could be. Intrigued by the combination of grace and fighting ability, I decided to take up tai chi. Bit by bit, I am learning about energy movements and body control and thinking about improving to the point where I can train with a sword or "push hands" with another student.

I'm also learning not to automatically reject freelance assignments that are different from anything I've ever done before. As my writer-friend Kelly Boyer Sagert once said, "I try not to confuse 'never having done it' with 'I can't do it.'" Just because I haven't done it before—just because I had never even *thought* of doing it before—doesn't mean that I can't or shouldn't do it now.

The fascinating aspect of all this challenge is that I feel more energized than I have ever felt before. I've learned that what Thomas Crum wrote in *Journey to Center* is true: "When we resist, we lose energy. When we choose to move forward, we gain energy."[2]

When I'm confronted by unpleasant circumstances or unexpected events, I try to remember that there are abilities in me that haven't yet come to the forefront and that this experience may be just what I need to bring it into the open. Change can lead to growth as long as we don't run from it.

The day will come when my suede boots will feel as comfortable and familiar to me as a pair of old slippers. Then I'll know that it's time to trade them in for something a little more daring, a little more "not me," and, in the process I'll learn that there is still more of me to find.

4

Keeping Faith

Flipping through channels on television one morning, I happened upon a commercial for an Irish tourism association. I had seen it thousands of times before, but that morning the opening line caught my attention: "Do you keep the promises you make to yourself?"

I was suddenly overwhelmed by a feeling of sadness and loss. I realized that of all the promises that I had made in my life, very few had been made to myself.

When was the last time *you* made a promise to yourself? And if you made one, did you keep it? I'm not talking about the "I promise to lose ten pounds/stop spending so much money/be nicer to my in-laws" kinds of promises. Those aren't really promises at all. They are behavior-oriented pledges so that we can become "better people." I'm talking about the kinds of promises that we make to our partners, our children, or our friends: "I promise to take you to the zoo." "I promise to help you color your hair." "I promise to [fill in the blank] because I know you will enjoy it." These kinds of promises have pleasure, joy, and just plain fun as the integral elements and make anticipation enjoyable because the recipient knows that you will honor the promise and that good times are ahead. These promises refresh the soul, invigorate the mind, and satisfy the body.

If we make these kinds of promises to others, why do we make them so rarely to ourselves? If such promises provide such positive results, we would be a happier group of people if we made and kept them for ourselves. But as psychologist, educator, and author Lawrence LeShan noted in *Meditating to Attain a Healthy Body Weight*, "Most of us are pretty good at keeping promises to others and pretty bad at keeping promises to ourselves."[1]

When I asked myself what promises I had made to myself in the last month, why I had made them, and if I had kept them, I realized that I had made far more promises to other people than I had to myself, and the ones that I had made just for me had been followed by qualifiers like "if I have time," "when I have a moment," and "as soon as my work is done."

It's not that there aren't things I want to do for myself; it's that there is always something seemingly more important that should be done first or someone who needs something done more than I do. My to-do list is 90 percent work-related and only 10 percent joy-driven, and that 10 percent is always subject to postponement. Even things that I do that *are* enjoyable have to be justified. For instance, I work out almost every day. I like exercising, and I rarely miss my workout time. But if I didn't *need* to exercise because of my mid-life weight gain and high cholesterol, I might be inclined to skip it. Somehow having a reason that doesn't take enjoyment into account makes it worth doing and worth making time for.

When did we stop making enjoyment a priority and when did activities have to have a good reason before we made them worth doing? Why do we feel guilty when we do break free and do something just for fun? Did we once put our enjoyment before another's wants and then have something bad happen as a result? When we crossed the line into adulthood, got married, had children, and started working, did we hear the unspoken but very clear message, "You can't just think of yourself. You have duties. The time for fun is over. Now and forevermore, you must be a responsible person."

Just for a moment, imagine that for the next twenty-four hours, everything you do has to benefit only you. You can eat whatever you want, go wherever you want, sleep until noon, or stay up past midnight. Be you-oriented and focus on activities that will bring you happiness and joy. Make a list of what you would do.

Are you finding it difficult? Is your first thought, "How selfish this sounds"? Do you struggle with each item on the list by starting to write it down and then deciding, "No, I couldn't do *that*!" Or maybe it's not so hard for you to record all your secret wants and desires because you figure that you won't really have to act on them and that you won't have to expose that "selfish" part of yourself to anyone but you.

Once after conducting a writing workshop at my local bookstore, a woman in her sixties came up to me and said, "I always wanted to write but never had the time," she said. "Thank you for giving me the time now to write."

I told her, "Don't thank me. I didn't give you anything. You gave it to yourself." For whatever reason, she had broken free for one night and had given herself permission to do what she wanted, to keep a promise she had made to herself God knows how many years earlier. Every now and then, I wonder if she kept on writing, if keeping that promise once made it easier to keep it a second time and then a third, or if the guilt got to her and she went back to doing her work instead of finding time for her joy.

Although it took her many years, author Loriann Hoff Oberlin was finally able to keep her promise to herself. When she was newly divorced with two young children, she knew, having written books on surviving separation and divorce and helping children through their anger, that pursuing graduate studies required resolving the twin challenges of logistics and finances. She decided to postpone her dream. Years later, with a better support system in place, she was finally able to pursue a master's in clinical community counseling, keeping the promise she had made to herself.

Pursuing the degree gave Loriann a new focus, new friends, and an abundance of ideas. She said that it was also about "doing something for myself, attaining a long-deferred goal—one of those 'shoulda, coulda, woulda' steps we all wistfully remember and can reframe, if only we put some action behind the dream."

In her essay "Windows of the Soul," author Jean Shinoda Bolen, MD, wrote, "When you recover or discover something that nourishes your soul and brings joy, care enough about yourself to make room for it in your life."[2] Honoring promises we have made to ourselves nourishes our spirit like food nourishes our body and enables us to live a balanced and fulfilled life.

5

The Cup without the Chip

As women, we are trained to take the smallest, oldest, or most damaged of anything. We choose the cup with the chip, the plate with the crack running through it, or the smallest piece of cake, thinking that it demonstrates unselfishness. But it actually sends the message that we deserve less, that what isn't good enough for anyone else is good enough for us. We routinely deny ourselves the riches that we hold out to others and then wonder why no one else wants to give us anything of value.

When my friend Betsy was a flight attendant—a career that involves long hours of running up and down narrow aisles—I bought her some cooling lotion for her feet. It was a simple, relatively inexpensive gift as a small token of our friendship. She put it away "for later," and it sat unused on her shelf for several months, even though her feet ached and burned after each flight. Then a houseguest used it one evening and raved about its cooling feel and wonderful scent. For a moment, Betsy was disconcerted. It wasn't that she minded her friend using it—she had told her to help herself to any toiletries she needed; it was that she suddenly realized that she had never used a gift intended for *her* enjoyment, a gift given in recognition of her value as a friend, because the moment was not right or because she hadn't done enough to deserve it.

We all share Betsy's attitude to one extent or another. To prove my point, I offer you a challenge: Tonight use some of the wonderful-smelling bath salts and powders you've received over the years, wear the satin panties and lace-trimmed nighties you had carefully put away for the right moments, and enjoy the soft, warm slippers you are saving for someday. *Today* is someday. This is the right moment.

When you serve dinner, serve yourself first. Take the juiciest piece of chicken, the biggest spoonful of mashed potatoes, or the corner of the cake with all the frosting. As you feel the guilt twinging in your soul, ask yourself, "Why don't I deserve this? Why is anyone else at the table more worthy of this than me?"

I'm not advocating total self-indulgence. Too much self-oriented behavior, like too much chocolate cake, can be detrimental to your health. But consider whether your tendency to consistently take less-than-the-best reflects unworthiness rather than unselfishness and self-dislike rather than self-sacrifice. "The relationships we have with the world are largely determined by the relationships we have with ourselves,"[1] Greg Anderson wrote in *The 22 Non-Negotiable Laws of Wellness*. If you don't believe that you are deserving of your own love, how will you be able to accept love from others?

This propensity to settle for less was a recurring problem for me in my relationships with men. Interestingly, I don't have this issue in my female friendships. Perhaps this is because I always subconsciously seek the company of women who validate my own worth and treat me—warts and all—as a person of value.

But with men I entered into relationships more for what I could do for them instead of for what they could bring into my life. I spent an inordinate amount of time demonstrating how helpful I could be, how I could answer all their needs, and how strong and competent I was. Then when they followed my lead and took without giving, I grew resentful of the one-way flow.

Whatever the reason for their behavior, I needed to confront why I felt the need to be needed, why I tried so hard to prove my worth to them and why, even when it was apparent that the relationship would never be the one I wanted, I still refrained from expressing my needs and focused instead on their happiness.

One evening I watched the 1990 movie *White Palace*, which stars Susan Sarandon as an older woman with a younger lover. When he gives her a hand-held vacuum cleaner, I (along with hundreds of other women, I'm sure) nodded my head in sympathy. And then I watched in amazement and envy when she does what I wouldn't: She throws it back at him and in no uncertain terms tells him what she thinks of a gift like that from a lover. I applauded her reaction but knew that I was incapable of doing the same.

I'm sure you have received your own "Dustbuster" gift. I'm ashamed to admit that, from one former lover, I received several over the years: a mulching blade for my lawn mower, a set of car ramps, and (the most hurtful gift of all because I was expecting an engagement ring) a box of lightbulbs. And each time a gift was presented, I said, "Oh, thank you very much. It's just what I wanted."

I couldn't even claim that he treated me well in other ways. His behavior throughout most of our relationship demonstrated that he did not see me as a person of value, someone to be cherished. His presents reflected how he felt about me. And I, accepting his valuation of me, continued to accept those presents.

I realized that I needed to take a hard look at myself and ask why I had to adopt the persona of a strong woman while never feeling secure enough to show my weaker side. Why did I give and give and give without ever asking for anything in return and then resent that my unspoken desires were not fulfilled?

My girlfriend Dianne, a wise, shoot-from-the-hip person, said that I must have been getting *something* from these kinds of relationships. Otherwise, why would I search them out? Subconsciously, I felt that I was better than the men I was involved with. I was stronger, more giving, and more loving. The martyr's crown never gleamed more brightly than when I put it on my own head, when I willingly put aside my own needs for someone else's wants.

But there would come a time in a relationship when I would notice that, in feeding the relationship, I was starving myself. The hunger pangs, at first only occasional twinges, would grow more frequent and insistent. When I would finally need to feed that hunger, the relationship would unravel because I was changing the rules, altering my expectations, and restricting my output while requiring more input. Inevitably I would fail to receive what I had belatedly realized I needed and deserved.

Who really was to blame: the men for not being able to give or me for choosing relationships with such men? Should my concentration be focused on fixing them or fixing myself?

I faced the fact that I couldn't expect to be in a reciprocating relationship until I had reached the point of believing that I deserved to be in one. I had to change. I had to be emotionally healthy if I wanted to be part of a healthy relationship. As Thomas Crum worte in *Journey to Center*, "At the root of a centered relationship are two people who are able to be centered with or without each other ... Relationships based on conditions derived from neediness and dependency aren't fulfilling. They don't support growth. They aren't nurturing. They aren't centered."[2]

For encouragement and support, Betsy gave me a set of Angelic Messenger Cards created by Meredith Young-Sowers. One card spoke of recognizing "the essential center of your life—your spirit and its ability to offer unconditional love and acceptance to yourself and all other living things."[3] Struck by this concept of self-love and self-acceptance, I realized that not only had the men in my life not truly loved me but I had indeed failed to love myself. I had confused self-love with selfishness and thought that a life of self-sacrifice was healthier than one in which I received as much love as I gave.

The road to what Crum calls "an aligned state of mind, unhindered by neediness"[4] has been a difficult one for me to travel and one marked with detours and potholes. But little by little I am finding it easier to take the cup without a chip and the plate that is whole and unmarred, and to give love to others without detracting from the love I can give to myself. No one can convince us that we are strong, capable, and worthy if we do not believe it ourselves. As Melody Beattie wrote in *The Language of Letting Go*, "The issue is not whether *others* see or care. The issue is whether we see and care about ourselves ... When we do, we have taken the first step toward removing ourselves as victims. We are on the way to self-responsibility, self-care, and change."[5]

And once we achieve a healthy sense of self-worth, it becomes a touchstone for every area of our life. We no longer desire relationships that fail to nurture, and we no longer measure our own worth by what we can sacrifice for another. Possibilities will become realities, opportunities will come forward, and dreams will become fulfilled in surprising ways when we realize that we deserve the best that life has to offer.

6

In the Moment

When my children were younger, life was crowded with errands, school functions, and doctor visits. As they grew up and left the house one after the other, I thought that it was my time to relax. I could work on my own projects and assignments or just enjoy newfound free time.

But I couldn't relax. My life seemed busier than ever, although I wasn't sure exactly what I was accomplishing. My days were focused on tomorrow's deadlines, next week's work, and next month's plans. I couldn't sit still long enough to read a book just for pleasure or go on my morning walk without calculating how much time it was taking away from other, more important obligations.

And I was tired, not physically but spiritually. I woke up tired and went to bed tired. The energy level that had sustained me through my twenties and thirties seemed to have dissipated now that I was heading into my fifties. I not only couldn't take the time to stop and smell the roses but I couldn't even tell if they were blooming!

I was experiencing what Wayne Muller described in *Sabbath: Remembering the Sacred Rhythm of Rest and Delight*: "The more our life speeds up, the more we feel weary, overwhelmed, lost. Our life and work rarely feel light, pleasant or healing. Instead, as it piles endlessly upon itself, the whole experience of being alive begins to melt into one enormous obligation."[1]

I was so busy living for the future that I had lost the ability to live in the moment, to find a measure of inner peace each day, and to simply enjoy being alive. It was clear that I needed to make a change.

I tried meditation, which, I had read, should be like floating in a pool of warm water. The instructions seemed simple: Don't try to go anywhere. Don't try to stop anything from drifting by. Just let the water support you, let the waves carry you where they will, and allow everything else to pass.

And I tried. I really did, sitting cross-legged in my room with the door closed, a candle lit, and my entire being focused on meditating. But I couldn't seem to stop my thoughts from swimming: Did anyone remember to run the dishwasher? Why is the furnace running so loud? Is the air cleaner due for maintenance? How am I going to pay this month's bills when I don't have my check from my always-delinquent editor? If I sit like this much longer, my legs will fall asleep!

It was a frustrating experience. I was trying too hard to find peace instead of sitting still and letting it come to me. I had turned my search for serenity into one more to-do task, forgetting that, as Harry Emerson Fosdick pointed out in *Light from Many Lamps*, peace can't be achieved on demand.[2]

Ironically, learning to relax and be in the moment would take just as much discipline as learning to run a household and handle my job. I was programmed to *do*; now I had to *be*. I needed to achieve a state of mindfulness that Joan Borysenko described in *Inner Peace for Busy Women*: "Coming back into the present moment ... to a state of natural mind that's present to what is without judgment, interpretation, or resistance."[3]

The diagnosis was made and the prescription was written, but where and when could I take my medicine? Everywhere I turned, everywhere I looked, there was something I was supposed to do. Bedroom, bathroom, office, kitchen—every physical space cried out for some kind of attention on my part—the antithesis to what I really needed to do.

To locate a quiet place, a place without distractions and diversions, I returned to a childhood routine of attending weekly services at a nearby church. This was not an easy schedule change, since for me Sunday had become a day of housework and grocery shopping, a day to play catch-up. God may have been able to create an entire world in six days, but somehow it took me all seven just to maintain my own little corner.

But I was willing to give it a try. I planned my morning so that I could arrive twenty minutes early to take advantage of the limited seating in the small chapel. What I hadn't taken into account was that, while I waited for Mass to begin, I had to sit there and do nothing. I couldn't talk, make a to-do list, write checks, or do anything but engage in purely reflective thought—something I had always claimed I didn't have time to do.

But now, each Sunday, I have time, and what was at first a frustrating experience (my mind kept reminding me how much time was being wasted just sitting there) has become a period of inner nourishment and tranquility. Until I finally had it, I didn't realize how important it was to have a moment of peace to let silence wash away the clamor that prevents us from listening to the voice within.

You don't need to attend religious services to find your peace. All you have to do is first make a conscious commitment to spending a set amount of time in a state of mindfulness and then make sure you don't sabotage it, deliberately or unconsciously. Treat it as a set appointment, that is sacrosanct and not subject to cancellation.

Decide what will work for you, based on your personality type. A darkened room with only a candle flame for illumination and soft music in the background is one option. Walking through a labyrinth, where your mind can run freely while your feet follow the established path, is another. Even those once-dreaded business trips can become your time for mindfulness. Invest in a Walkman, bring along some calming music (New Age, classical, or whatever works for you), and let your mind travel where it needs to go.

You may find, as I did, that while you can shut out the outside world, quieting the voices in your head is much harder. You might suffer from what my yoga teacher, Tina, calls "Monkey Mind."

If you've ever visited the primate section at the zoo, you've probably noticed how well developed monkeys' verbal skills are. Chattering, screeching, and almost barking, monkeys can talk up a storm with little or no encouragement. When you suffer from Monkey Mind, it's like having a cage full of those creatures in your head, all chattering away. While it's difficult to control the monkey noise in your head, some people find it easier to let it go in one ear and out the other. Eventually you'll see, as I did, that the more often you practice mindfulness, the easier it becomes to find that still place inside. We are, after all, creatures of habit. If we do a task often enough, it becomes almost second nature.

While it's a good idea to establish a regular routine of meditative practice, don't overlook the unexpected experiences that can generate the same sense of wisdom and inner peace. A few years ago, my friend Cindy was struggling with a hard career decision. Needing to take time off to think things through, she took a vacation to the Grand Canyon and spent twelve days rafting, camping under the stars, exploring the canyon, and, more importantly, being inaccessible by e-mail, phone, or any other kind of communication. As Cindy put it, "I had a true break from my normal life. The experience showed me that the work I was doing was not right for me after all, and that I had lost the sense of balance in my life. I started to look for a change, and within two months had quit that job and moved back to where I had grown up, taking a role in my parents' company. It's been almost five years since then, and I'm still glad I made the change. I still struggle to have balance in life, but I feel much happier and fulfilled."

By removing herself from her normal environment, Cindy quieted the monkey chatter enough to hear the truth in the stillness. Once we take the time to sit in silence and learn to ignore the outside distractions and the internal chatter, we will hear the message from our spirit. We carry our own truth within ourselves, but to hear it we must create pockets of stillness and mindfulness.

Part II:
In the Midst
of Change

7

Taking the First Step

What is it about decision making that compels us to want to turn and run? Maybe this isn't true in every instance, but I defy you to find anyone who looks forward to weighing alternatives and then picking the better of the two—or three or four. Changing jobs, buying a house, picking a mate, or even altering our hair color can generate that familiar butterflies-in-the-stomach feeling that portends possible disaster.

Maybe we fear decision making because, deep down inside, we don't really believe that we are qualified to come up with the right solution for ourselves. It's not that we don't know what's wrong in our life or when a decision is required. The problem lies in choosing the *right* solution. We often go to others for advice, but this can further compound the difficulty because their solution may not necessarily be the one that is right for us.

Each one of us has his or her own standards, limitations, and situations that we will agree to and others that we won't even consider. These may be vastly different from those of our family or friends. It is unreasonable and detrimental to our own future to allow anyone else to make a decision for us. We can solicit advice and weigh the responses, but in the end, the choice must be ours because we are the one most affected. As the saying goes, "the buck stops here," only in this case, the buck is both the decision and its consequence. You can let someone else—a friend, family member, doctor, minister, or therapist—tell you what to do. You can even decide to do as you are told. But in the end you and you alone will experience the consequences of that decision.

So how can we make healthy decisions that will move us forward? First we must step back and look objectively at the situation. We have to disregard how we wish things would have been or how we wish other people would have behaved. The past can't be altered or rewritten. Instead we need to identify our desired end result. If we know how we want things to be, then we can work backwards and decide how we can produce that result.

For instance, if you are unhappy with your job, you realize that it will never give you the satisfaction or fulfillment that you desire. You may want something different, something better, more challenging, and more rewarding. You could spend hours, days, or even weeks focusing on all that's wrong with your present position. You could even fixate on the people (boss, co-workers, clients) who make the situation unpleasant. But will that change anything? Will it improve the situation? Will you be able to handle it better? Probably not. And you'll undoubtedly bore your friends and family to death with your complaints. As Dennis Wholey pointed out in *The Miracle of Change*, "Sooner or later we must accept life's reality that we can't change anyone—ever—and trying to change situations that can't be changed is even crazier."[1]

What you must do is look beyond the present circumstance. If you weren't where you are, with the person you are with, or doing what you are doing, what other reality could you envision? Who else could you be? What else could you be?

Then ask yourself if you are willing to do what you need to do to create that new reality. You might picture a life of luxury on a forty-foot yacht, but if you're not willing to work the hours required to make it happen, you'd better settle for a model ship on your bookshelf.

After working for several years in someone else's company, I was itching to strike out on my own as a freelance writer. Although there is something to be said for letting higher-ups worry about the IRS, business insurance, and payroll requirements, my job was unfulfilling. And since I couldn't change the conditions of my job, I needed to change where I was and what I was doing.

From previous experience, I knew that self-employment had its downside. What motivated me was the vision of what I wanted to be doing. I pictured my new life, how I would earn my living, what kind of writing I would do, and who my customers would be. With that picture firmly in my mind, I gave notice and joined the ranks of entrepreneurs. On days when things aren't quite matching up to the life I had envisioned, I pull that picture out of storage, look at it again, and gain the courage to continue, certain that I am on the right path.

What if you're afraid that the decision you make will be the wrong one? The more you weigh the alternatives, the more confused and uncertain you will become, until you are caught in a mental tar pit of indecision. As Thomas Crum described in *Journey to Center*, you are employing F.E.A.R., "Fantasy Experienced As Real." "When you are paralyzed with fear," he wrote, "you are literally stuck in time. You are worried about a future possibility based on a real (or imagined) past, thus the acronym F.E.A.R."[2]

Even if the new job is worse than the old one, you still have a choice: stay the course and see if things improve or move on. And if you choose to move on, then you have another decision: return to your former employer (if that's an option) or go somewhere new; stay in your present occupation or explore a different one; or stay in the same area or move somewhere else.

Even if the first decision you make doesn't turn out right, you always get another chance to make another one. Life itself is really a succession of choices: Path A or Path B, Door Number One or Door Number Two. In the end, using the right criteria to make our choices is more important than whether we made the right decision. If something doesn't work out, we always have another chance to correct it. We can step back, evaluate the situation, determine what went wrong, and then make another choice.

Not making a choice is a choice in and of itself, but what we shouldn't ever do is choose *not* to decide. Even if, as Robyn Davidson wrote in *Meditations for Women Who Do Too Much*, "the most difficult part of any endeavor is taking the first step, making the first decision,"[3] it is still preferable to standing there at the crossroads, watching your future leave you behind. As Theodore Roosevelt once said, "In any moment of decision the best thing you can do is the right thing, the next best thing is the wrong thing, and the worst thing you can do is nothing."[4]

When a decision is needed, when a change is called for, we must take action. Otherwise, no forward movement is possible.

"We are given one life," said General Omar Nelson Bradley, "and the decision is ours whether to wait for circumstances to make up our mind, or whether to act, and in acting, to live."[5]

8

The Act of Mindful Choosing

In my world there is a surfeit of things to do. The ones that are completed first are the squeakiest wheels: complete that magazine assignment, redesign a brochure for my business, fold that last load of laundry, set out the final row of tomato plants. If I try to postpone these tasks in favor of work that seems less necessary or less important, the guilt is almost more than I can bear.

A therapist I used to see called this "should-ing on myself." I should iron those shirts because they will look better when my husband wears them. I should call my friend because she will feel hurt that I didn't make time for her. I should babysit my grandson because I know how difficult it is to have a free moment when you're a young mother. The prevailing sentiment, of course, is that I will be guilty of self-ishness if I put my own desires ahead of "real work" and other obligations.

When guilt determines what gets done first, I, like most women, tend to push the enjoyable tasks aside in favor of required work. I "should" myself into an endless daily round of labors and am unable to make time for activities that bring me a greater sense of joy and fulfillment. As children, we were often told that being a grown-up means doing work we dislike because it has to get done. To some extent, this is true. If we want the necessities of life available to us and our families, we have to earn money. If we want to live in a clean home, we have to scrub the tub and toilet. If we want fresh-smelling clothes, we must empty the laundry hamper and wash clothes. If we want to eat, we need to make a grocery list, stand in line at the store, and then return home and prepare the meal.

The problem arises when this is all we do, when our life becomes an endless exercise wheel of tasks that no sooner gets completed than requires doing again, when a sense of personal achievement and fulfillment is absent from most or all our life, and when we begin to resent or feel discontent with how our time is spent. Our lives become lopsided, weighted heavily on the side of duty, because we failed to heed Robert Fulghum's sensible recommendation to "live a balanced life—learn some and think some and draw and paint and sing and dance and play and work every day some."[1] But how can we, as responsible, productive members of society, and our family in particular, justify setting aside time for projects that might bring us *only* a sense of satisfaction or completion?

Our first duty is to live a balanced, fulfilled life. Spending an evening stitching our needlepoint instead of darning socks or serving boxed macaroni-and-cheese instead of making it from scratch so that we have time to read an enjoyable book should not be considered as self-indulgent. In fact, we owe it to ourselves. Author Barbara Sher reminded us in her book *I Could Do Anything If I Only Knew What It Was*, "'Doing your own thing' is a generous act. Being gifted creates obligations, which means you owe the world your best effort at the work you love. You too are a natural resource."[2]

This doesn't mean that your artistic talents have to rival Mary Cassatt's to justify spending time on them or that every book you read must provide food for an assignment instead of simply for your soul. It doesn't even mean that other people have to acknowledge what you have done to make it worth doing. When we nourish ourselves and experience joy in the act of doing instead of relief from completing a task, that contentment spills over into every other area of our lives, making those within our sphere of influence beneficiaries of our mindful choosing. We are more open and loving, calmer, and more centered.

Mindful choosing is consciously deciding how to spend the precious and limited time we have here on this earth. It means that we don't automatically rush to fill our days with tasks without first evaluating their importance and necessity. It means that we review our choices on a daily basis, ensuring that the "shoulds" do not consistently outweigh the "wants," and that we spend some minutes or hours on activities that utilize the best and most unique aspects of our inner selves.

We are more than the clean clothes on our backs, the paychecks in our pockets, and the mother/daughter/friend identities that we have assumed. We are most uniquely ourselves, with gifts and abilities that only we possess and can express. And when we consistently bury these parts of ourselves under a mound of "shoulds" and "must-dos," we risk suffocating the essence of who we are.

I have been freelancing for some years now, and while I enjoy my work and feel a sense of satisfaction in creating a company out of nothing more than a talent for words, I felt that there was more inside of me. I had more to offer and was frustrated because there simply wasn't time to explore it. But in time I recognized that I alone was responsible for how my time was spent, and if I was so dissatisfied with what was happening, it was up to me to change it. It wasn't an easy task, because I had been programmed to put my job before all else. The transition from automatic pilot to mindful choosing came when I began to work on a book of essays. As one essay became two and then three and four, I felt more in touch with my inner self than I had in a long time. The more time I spent writing and exploring my inner world, the less frustrated I felt when I had to close my essay file and open the client ones. I had struck a balance between my need to earn an income and my need to express my individuality.

I like to think of goals in terms of the price we pay to achieve them. One of my favorite quotes is from writer Toni Cade Bambara: "Anything of value is going to cost you something."[3] When the goal we are striving for is a healthy one, the price is affordable, and we are as excited by the journey toward the goal as we are about the prospect of reaching it. Think about a time when you were engaged in a project that you truly enjoyed. You wanted to do the work, you enjoyed it, and you threw yourself into it wholeheartedly; and when you weren't actually working on it, you talked about it. Long after the project was completed, you could relive the enjoyment simply by recalling what you had done. In every aspect, it was a fulfilling experience.

In contrast, when you have to undertake a task that is boring, repetitive, or unfulfilling, the very thought of it is draining. Your mood sours, your attitude becomes negative, and when the project is finally completed, you feel as though you had been let out of prison.

Unfortunately this is how we live our lives far too often. If we assume that our adult life should be spent on tasks that don't bring us joy or fulfillment, then we will summarily reject any idea that even hints of enjoyment and only choose goals that are clothed in necessity. And we will pay a high price for something that doesn't bring us a good return on our investment; we will invest our energy and our time in a draining proposition, instead of on one that will rejuvenate us and fill our mental and emotional bank accounts.

Someone once said that unhappiness is in not knowing what we want and killing ourselves to get it, and it's quite true. How many people reach the end of their career or their life and regret how they used the time they had been allotted? Perhaps the key to happiness, satisfaction, or fulfillment (whichever word you prefer) is making certain that we truly want what we are purchasing with our time and energy. Then the value far outweighs the cost, and the rewards more than compensate for the energy we've expended.

Using mindful choosing requires a sense of awareness to where your time and energy are being directed. It means giving voice to those hitherto unexpressed desires and then finding ways to make them a reality. It means recognizing that you alone are responsible for how your time is spent. Mindful choosing can be frightening. It's easier to blame others when we feel unfulfilled or overwhelmed or to reject suggestions for finding time for ourselves as impractical or selfish. But as long as we function on automatic pilot instead of exercising mindful choosing, we will never find the treasure that lies within us.

9

The Mouth of the Tiger

I first heard the expression "going into the mouth of the tiger and coming back" from Dick Holmstrom, a man I had serendipitously met while on a plane to California. It's a Vietnam-era Navy expression referring to taking a high-speed vessel up the narrow Mekong River in search of heavily armed enemy soldiers, engaging them in battle, and returning safely back to base.

"Going into the mouth of the tiger" means taking up a challenge, regardless of the potential negative outcome. It requires you to leave your comfort zone, which is a scary proposition but one that can have wonderful rewards or offer the greatest potential for self-development.

There is no shortage of challenges in life. The question isn't where they are but how we handle them. Do we figuratively load our weapons, board our vessel, and prepare for battle? Or do we run the other way, more afraid of what might go wrong than excited about what might go right?

In my work I have interviewed a number of women whose lives have been less than smooth. One woman had gone from single parenthood to an unhappy marriage and poverty before divorcing her husband and successfully starting her own company. Another woman had spent years working as a hospice nurse, until the physical and emotional toll became too great. She turned her talents to the kitchen and now markets delicious condiments nationwide. Both women, and many more like them, had survived unexpected trials of life and chose paths that ultimately brought them fulfillment and joy.

Another woman who has gone into the mouth of the tiger and emerged, perhaps not unscathed but certainly victorious, is my friend Dianne. She left an abusive marriage to found Educating Against Domestic Violence. Along the way, she wrote the enlightening and inspirational *Whose Face Is In the Mirror?* which has helped countless abused woman take control of their lives.

My sister-in-law Shirley has been beset by the tiger of ill health. He sprang from his hiding place and has wounded her repeatedly. But although her body has been weakened, her spirit has remained strong. She has vanquished the tiger, not by overcoming her illnesses but by refusing to allow bitterness, anger, or sorrow overwhelm her and control the rest of her life.

In my life I have had my own tigers to battle. There was the career tiger who roared at me when I decided to follow my desire to be a freelance writer. He peered at me over the shoulders of potential clients, hissing that I could never satisfy their needs. With claws extended, he jumped out of envelopes containing bills, waiting to seize what little money I had, growling that he would leave me destitute.

Then there was the emotional tiger, the one who padded ominously behind me when relationships failed and stalked me when my parents had life-threatening health problems. This tiger hissed, "You'll never be able to get through this" and "No one will ever love you again." He clawed at me in the form of painful words from someone I once trusted or in the shape of memories that recalled the one I had lost.

Is it the tiger we fear or our own ability to fight him? Is fear the enemy or our own self-doubt? Is the low growling we hear the tiger or our own negative thoughts? Are the messages in the growls fact-based or are they false assumptions? Listen to the tiger and then ask yourself if what he says is true. If the statement reflects your personal self-beliefs rather than objective reality, you needn't enter the bush to find the tiger. He's not in there; he's waiting in your mind.

There was a time in my life when I felt incapable of forward movement. I had lost almost all hope of things going right, and, worse, doubted my ability to deal with the situation at hand. The only thing I felt confident about was failure. As I mentally explored options, a voice inside my head kept saying, "This won't work. Turn back, turn back." I went to bed with my fears, and when I drank my morning coffee, they joined me at the breakfast table. Finally I reached the point where I thought that if there were that many reasons pointing to failure, I shouldn't even try.

Then I found a book that addressed my fears and declawed the tiger. In *Feel the Fear and Do It Anyway*, Susan Jeffers broke all fears into three levels and concluded, "At the bottom of every one of your fears is simply the fear that you can't handle whatever life may bring you."[1]

It was a novel thought that there was one enemy to vanquish instead of an army, only one tiger in the bush, not an onslaught. I realized that all those feelings of fear didn't mean that my idea was a bad one. Fear itself wasn't even the problem; it was that I was allowing my fear to direct my course of action. I was operating under the mistaken belief that fear was keeping me from danger when it was really keeping me from growth.

I took heart from two of Jeffers's empowering statements: "The fear will never go away as long as I continue to grow" and "pushing through fear is less frightening than living with the underlying fear that comes from a feeling of helplessness."[2]

I kept Jeffers's book by my bedside, and every night I read through it, highlighting phrases that addressed my concerns and doubts. And gradually, as I moved forward, accepted the challenge, and chose to give it my best shot, I felt stronger and more alive. Once I faced the tiger, I stopped reacting and started acting. I made a conscious decision not to be a victim of circumstances and began to create my own.

While going into the mouth of the tiger is fraught with uncertainty, refusing to fight means that we will lose the opportunity to learn something about ourselves, to challenge ourselves, and to grow. What we gain from one battle ultimately fortifies us for the next. By challenging the tiger and facing our fears, we become stronger, more empowered, and better able to move forward in our life.

10

Yoga Stork Pose

The Stork pose in yoga looks deceptively simple. You begin by transferring all your weight to one leg and then raise the other, placing your foot on the side of your calf, knee, or, ideally, your upper thigh. Your hands are clasped in prayer position, and your eyes are looking forward, focused on one spot. The whole goal is to keep yourself in balance while breathing deeply and rhythmically.

"You must concentrate," the instructor had said. "Keep your eyes focused on one spot to maintain your balance." And she was right. The minute I let my eyes—and mind—start to wander, my balance wavers, my posture slips, and both feet are flat on the ground.

This happens in my life as well, more often than I care to admit. I am moving forward, fairly certain of where I want to go and how to get there and then—*bam!* I find myself on a totally different path, teetering on the brink of disaster. I've lost my focus, and, in doing so, lost my balance as well. As much as I would like to blame it on someone else or on external circumstances, the fact of the matter is that I chose to look away from my goal and let my mind wander and therefore lost my concentration.

We all do this to one extent or another. Some of us lose focus out of a sense of altruism. We see someone else's need and want to fill it. We see helplessness and want to be helpful. There is nothing necessarily wrong with that, but the problem arises when we are so busy doing for others that we forget to focus on ourselves. The outflow of energy depletes our own internal resources. That's when we need to stop and ask ourselves if we have crossed the line from doing *what* we can to doing *more* than we should. And sometimes we lose our focus to others because we are convinced that we alone have the right answers. We stop working on our own lives and start fixing everyone else's, robbing people of the chance to make and implement their own decisions.

Fear of failure can also unbalance us. Confronted with a challenge or life change, we start to worry: What if we can't handle it? What if we disappoint others? What if we fail? Fear of success can be just as debilitating. We enjoy a certain security in maintaining the status quo. Once we surpass that level, the bar has been raised. People will expect more from us, and we'll expect more from ourselves. And we'll no longer have an excuse or justification to do less. We've shown what we are capable of, and now we have to reach that height again and again.

Regardless of the cause, the point is that we lose our balance. When we take the concentration that is supposed to keep us upright and send it to someone or something else, we fall. When our concentration is distracted by our negative thoughts and fears, we fall.

How can we keep our balance in a world that is constantly pulling and tugging at us? How can we keep our eyes focused on our own goals when people around us may be calling, "Look at me! Help me! I'm falling!" or if our mind is whispering, "You can't do it" or "You'll regret it if you succeed"?

1. *We must first make certain that the goal is the right one for us.* We should truly desire the outcome for the right reasons. We should want to stop smoking not because our spouse wants us to but because we truly want to have healthy lungs. We should want to stop cheating not because we are afraid of getting caught but because we acknowledge that it's wrong for us. We should want to change jobs or seek

self-employment not because someone else said we should do it but because we know, in our heart, that it's the right decision for us.

2. *The motivation must be a positive force, not a negative one.* We need to make the change not because we are afraid of what will happen if we don't but because we want to make it. As Peter McWilliams pointed out in *You Can't Afford the Luxury of a Negative Thought*, "Positive thoughts (joy, happiness, fulfillment, achievement, worthiness) have positive results (enthusiasm, calm, well-being, ease, energy, love). Negative thoughts (judgment, unworthiness, mistrust, resentment, fear) produce negative results (tension, anxiety, alienation, anger, fatigue)."[1]

3. *We must be supportive of ourselves.* Why do some people succeed in self-employment when so many fail? It isn't because they are smarter, richer, or in a better economic environment but because they believe in themselves. They wake up in the morning, look in the mirror, and tell themselves, "You can do it!" They applaud themselves when they succeed at signing a client, and they don't berate themselves when they fail; instead they look at failure as a learning experience.

4. *We need to surround ourselves with people who support our decision.* When I am in yoga class, I often notice that we fall victim to the "domino effect." We are all perfectly balanced, hands clasped, eyes forward. Then one person

wavers. Then another. Before long, we are all teetering, and a few have lost the position entirely. Like yawning, unbalancing is contagious.

When we focus on our goal, we need to have like-minded people around us. They don't necessarily have to have the same target in mind but they do have to be equally committed to reaching their destination. Among my close circle of friends, only one other person is a writer, but all my friends are very focused, committed individuals. They are self-driven people who move forward even when the way is strewn with obstacles. They are positive thinkers who have established healthy goals for themselves that are in line with their own attitudes and ethics. Their energy feeds my energy, as mine feeds theirs. Metaphorically, we are all standing balanced, in perfect Stork pose.

5. *Watch out for distractions.* For some reason, my cats are drawn to me when I am practicing yoga. If I'm upside down in Downward Dog, Sonny walks back and forth in front of my face and brushes my nose with his tail. Or if I am preparing for Cobra, BK leaps onto my shoulder. It's pretty tough to keep your concentration with a twelve-pound feline purring in your ear!

In the same way, you might find yourself plagued with people who want your attention right now, events that demand treatment immediately, or circumstances that require decisions ASAP. Sometimes you have to break your focus—just for the moment—and deal with what is going on. Other times the distraction can wait. You need to determine what's right for you. It's OK to say, "I am keeping my eyes focused on the goal. That problem (or event or situation) is not mine to deal with. I need to stay balanced."

6. *Recheck your position.* Try to stand on one leg. Notice how your body is constantly undergoing tiny shifts: tendons lengthening, muscles flexing, joints relaxing. You may feel yourself going too far to the right, and almost before you recognize the problem, your body begins to realign itself.

In life you need to periodically check your position and make sure that your focus is still on the right goal, because sometimes the goal shifts and we must shift with it. Sometimes circumstances change and we need to surrender one dream because it is no longer within reach or within the same reach.

Life is an endless balancing act that is even more difficult when Fate sends little ripples into it. Then we have to work harder to keep our eyes on the target if we don't want to waver. And if we do waver or lose our balance entirely, we must take a deep breath and rebalance. There is no shame in falling. As actress Mary Pickford observed, "You may have a fresh start any moment you choose . . . this thing we call 'failure' is not the falling down, but the staying down."

We all need to find our balance and our focus. We were put here on this earth for very specific reasons: To live our life as fully and completely as we can. To utilize the abilities we have to move forward. To set healthy, fulfilling goals and then do all we can to reach them. And, when we falter, to once more find our focus, achieve our balance, and go on.

11

One Thing at a Time

I am a confirmed list maker. Every day, pen in hand, I open my schedule book and detail tasks that are most in need of being completed. Like the rabbit in *Alice's Adventures in Wonderland*, I am always thinking of my schedule, how much I have to accomplish, and how little time there is in which to do it, which frequently pushes me into multitasking overdrive.

You know what I mean: you wash dinner dishes while you catch up with your friends on the phone. You fold clothes while quizzing your child on French nouns and verbs. You use drive time to resolve disputes between your children. You add items to your household shopping list while fielding client calls or your boss's demands. And each time you do double-duty, you applaud yourself for your organizational skills.

Does this sound like your day? Even now, while you are reading this, is some part of your mind thinking of what you have to do later today, tonight, or tomorrow? Is your brain buried under a mass of mental sticky notes, making it difficult to think clearly? Take the advice Sarah Ban Breathnach offered in *Simple Abundance: A Daybook of Comfort and Joy*: "Today, we must start to recover our sanity. The way we do this is to concentrate slowly on completing one task at a time."[1]

How can you tell when you are suffering from multi-tasking excess? Here are some key indicators:

- You pull into a parking lot and realize that you don't remember any details of the drive.
- Dinner is over but you don't recall the taste of the food or even eating it.
- You have conversations with friends or family members but later can't remember what was said.
- When you only do two things at once, you feel as though you are slacking off.
- When someone asks what you did the day before, you have to consult your datebook.

There are times when multitasking is unavoidable or even necessary. All too often, the multitude of responsibilities we bear makes it essential that we function as efficiently as possible, and sometimes that means finding ways of doing more than one activity at the same time. But when we multitask as a matter of course or habit, we rob ourselves of a sense of accomplishment or pride in what we have done because we are still doing something else. We don't experience a feeling of completion because there is still so much on our to-do list. We confuse quantity with quality, thinking that the number of tasks completed or obligations fulfilled is more important than the degree of excellence or thoroughness to which the work is done. And we wonder why we feel a pervading sense of exhaustion coupled by a sense that we just aren't working hard enough, fast enough, or well enough because, if we were, wouldn't we be done by now?

Despite all the checkmarks next to completed items on my to-do list, I felt increasingly frustrated and dissatisfied. I knew that my work was not at the level I wanted it to be, my children complained that I never really listened to them ("I told you that already, Mom! Didn't you listen?" was a frequent refrain), and it was becoming less and less intrinsically satisfying to be Super-woman. I had to do something different, extreme, and decisive. I had to take a 180-degree turn in how I handled my life.

If it's time for you to adopt the dictum "less is more" when it comes to your workload, try this three-step process that will take you from being the Queen of Multitasking to a Super Single-Tasker.

1. *For twenty-four hours, do just one thing at a time.* No multitasking allowed. No answering e-mails while talking on the phone or reading the news while drinking your coffee. Award each task, large or small, its own time for completion, granting it a singular importance on your daily to-do list.

You may find, as I did, that this is much harder than expected. In my case, the challenge started with my morning walk, when a babble of voices in my head usually competed for attention: the as-yet undetermined lead for the article due that day, the possible outcomes of a family member's health problems, the housework that I needed to attend to the moment I got back. As soon as one of these thoughts surfaced, I would tell myself, "One thing at a time. Right now, you are on a walk. Concentrate on that." Although that intruder would leave, another would soon take its place, and once again, I had to send it packing. I was amazed at how much unwelcome company I had taken along with me on other mornings.

After I finished my experiment, I realized how often I did two or more things at a time and how little I remembered of the doing, living each day in a state of semi-awareness that was psychologically unsatisfying. And I understood that while multitasking may sometimes be necessary it is not a constant requirement of a productive life.

2. *Take the process to another level by pausing after each task to show appreciation to the person who accomplished it: you.* For

instance, after you fold that last basket of laundry, recognize the commitment involved in providing your family with fresh, clean clothes. When you turn in a project at work, value the professional skills you possess that contributed to the company. No one else may know or care about what you did, but that doesn't matter. Value your labors and your many different roles. If you don't, how can you expect anyone else to?

3. *Move from multitasking through single-tasking to zero-tasking.* Do *nothing*—no action of any kind. I'm talking about sit-still-and-be-at-one-with-the-universe nothing.

For many of us, this might prove to be the biggest challenge. I can hear you now: "Do nothing? I don't have time to do nothing! My family/job/world would come crashing to a halt if I did nothing!"

Relax. I'm not advocating that you quit your job, abdicate your personal responsibilities, and live under a tree with nothing but the clothes on your back. But what I do want you to do is interject little moments of inaction into your life. Each time you complete a task, imagine that you've reached an intersection where the light has just turned red. Stop and recognize where you are at that moment—at the corner of What-I-Just-Did Avenue and What-I-Will Do-Next Street—before rushing down the next road.

You may find, as I did, that the idea of stopping or even slowing down is at odds with your normal behavior. But taking a brief pause—a Breath Break—can actually result in an increase in energy. We are giving ourselves—our mind, body, and spirit—the chance to breathe, refresh, and reinvigorate. Try it now: for the next sixty seconds, put down this book and do nothing. Sit still. Breathe. Relax. Don't think. Don't plan. Don't file your nails or your paperwork. Stop. Center yourself. Breathe.

Fill your body with the deepest breath you can take in, hold it, and then release it gently. There's no magic number of inhalations and exhalations, no target to strive for—that would be turning your Breath Break into a task. Just sit quietly for one minute and let yourself be.

Time's up. Did you find it difficult to take that break, even for such a short time? Did you keep stealing glances at your watch, convinced that sixty seconds must have passed already, that you couldn't possibly have only been inactive for just half that time? If so, that illustrates the speed you've been moving at.

Now check your breathing. Is it a little slower and a little deeper? Does your body feel even the tiniest bit more relaxed? Just imagine how much calmer, more centered, and more energized you would feel if you had stretched it another minute or two or three. Paradoxically, the more often you pause for Breath Breaks, the more you will be able to accomplish.

Mihaly Csikszentmihalyi pointed out in *Finding Flow: The Psychology of Engagement with Everyday Life* that there are limits on what we can do and feel, and ignoring those limits "leads to denial and eventually to failure. To achieve excellence, we must first understand the reality of the everyday, with all its demands and potential frustrations."[2]

Datebooks and calendars, to-do lists, and deadlines are unavoidable aspects of modern life. We must make a conscious choice to do one thing at a time, appreciate our own achievements to our best ability, and, most importantly, take the time to refresh and replenish our souls. We will then achieve a life measured not by quantity but by quality, not by tasks completed but by moments truly lived.

12

The Wings of Change

"Change begets change,"[1] Charles Dickens once said. Perhaps that is why we don't embrace it quite as often and as whole-heartedly as we should. We may need change to enter our lives; perhaps at some level, we even desire it. But, to para-phrase St. Augustine, we are wont to say, "Lord, let me change—but not yet."

Change can occur in a variety of areas: physically, emo-tionally, and spiritually. We can have a change of jobs, a change of address, a change of spouse, or a change of heart. And any one of these changes can have a correlating effect on other areas of our lives. A person makes one alteration and somehow that change sets in motion a whole series of other changes—and those changes ripple outward to affect relationships with friends and family.

One familiar example is that of a woman who is dissatisfied with her appearance and alters her hair color, clothing, or weight. Her spouse, confronted with this new person, may dislike or resent the change, perhaps even going so far as to leave her for someone more like the old wife.

Or if a man who has spent his whole life in the corporate environment strikes out for entrepreneur-land, those left behind to punch the time clock may resent his freedom and choose to undermine his confidence.

Getting married or having children can also spark less-than-supportive reactions from friends and family. It's not that those around us wish us ill or want us to fail. Their reactions are often generated by love, because they love us and want the best for us. They want us to be safe and don't want us to take chances that could turn out badly or cause us pain. Like parents watching a baby learn to walk, they want to protect us from the bumps and bruises that go along with flexing new muscles and undertaking new challenges.

Sometimes the negative feedback has less to do with the change that we make, and is more about the change that the other person needs to make. When one person makes a major life change, it shines a bright light on everyone else's decisions. Those around us may feel a need to justify their life choices when confronted by the path we are taking, especially if it represents for them the road not taken.

How do we handle it when we are ready to move forward yet find those we love and trust trying to turn us away from the path we have chosen? How do we strike a balance between honoring their feelings and following our own? And what about those uncomfortable moments, those dark times of the soul when we wonder if the others may be right, that this change is misguided at best and dangerous at worst?

If you are planning to make a change, first list all the desirable aspects that may result from it and then the work you will have to do to make it happen. A slimmed-down figure requires modifications in eating and exercise, a new baby requires a surrender of the carefree lifestyle, and marriage demands commitment. If you are looking only at the positive aspects of the change but not the requirements of achieving and maintaining it, perhaps you need to reconsider your decision.

Consider your track record: do you have a tendency to rush into new schemes, only to lose steam partway through the endeavor? Is the landscape of your life littered with half-finished projects or abandoned goals? If follow-through is a problem for you, then you must consider the possibility that you either lack discipline or fail to be fully committed. These tendencies are death knells for successful change.

When we evaluate others' opinions, we should consider their track record as well. What has been their response in the past when we have tried something new? Have they been honest but supportive or only too ready throw cold water on all our plans? Have they urged us to follow our own dreams or demand that, to keep their approval, we adhere to their way of doing things?

Over the years, I have made many decisions that have generated major life changes. Some have worked out, while others have failed. Through it all, my family members have supported my efforts, even when they questioned the wisdom of my actions. Because of their encouragement and faith in me (if not always in my plans), I am more willing to try something new.

This is not to say that we should delay change until everyone agrees with our plans. As Neale Donald Walsch said, "So long as you're still worried about what others think of you, you are owned by them. Only when you require no approval from outside yourself can you own yourself."[2] This is *our* life, after all—we are the ones who will suffer the consequences of our actions or inactions. If we are willing, as Thoreau said, to leap into the dark to our success, then we should not let the opinions of others impede us.

As for our own self-doubt, we must remember that change generates fear simply because it forces us to move out of our comfort zone and into new and unfamiliar territory. Of course, we will be nervous, ill at ease, or at times paralyzed with fear. That's normal and to be expected.

"Change is upsetting," said author Meredith Young-Sowers, "because the unknown has no discernible texture, no familiar faces, no assurances of success. When you are unable to ascertain what is coming into your life through the mist of change, it is easy and natural to be afraid."[3]

While we may feel afraid, uncomfortable, or insecure, we shouldn't let those unpleasant emotions stop us from moving forward on our chosen path. The best antidote for fear is knowledge. The more we know about the road ahead, the more confident we will feel about our journey. As much as possible, explore all the aspects of the change you are making. What will you have to learn? What abilities will you have to develop? How will this change affect others in your life? Have you undertaken the work necessary to prepare yourself for the new life you are creating?

Think of the butterfly. Once an earthbound caterpillar, it remains inside its chrysalis until it has completed its transformation. Only then will it emerge. But that is only half of the process. Once outside its shelter, the butterfly must exercise its wings until the blood flows through every tiny capillary. Only when the wings are fully developed is the butterfly then ready to catch the wind. In the same way, we, too, need to stretch our wings if we want to soar to new heights.

13

Flexing Your Adaptability Muscle

"Change is good." "I like change." "Change is my friend."

I've been saying those phrases to myself quite a bit recently. It seems that every time I turn around, something new and unexpected is happening. It's not that I want to live a life totally devoid of unanticipated events; I would just like a break between them, a chance to catch my breath and get ready for the next round coming my way.

Trouble may come in threes, but for many of us, I suspect that change has no special number. Life rolls along, quietly and serenely, and then suddenly we are expected to deal with a series of unforeseen, and possibly undesired, circumstances that put us into a high-stress state.

Last year started off great for me. It looked like it was finally going to be my year. My corporate clients were inundating my e-mail in-box and mailbox with new assignments, my book projects were moving merrily along, I had sold an article to a major magazine, and agents, editors, and publishers were at least commenting favorably on my writing. Of course, all this inspired me to work harder than ever. "Make hay while the sun shines," the old adage goes, and I knew all too well that the freelance well could dry up at any moment, leaving my wallet thirsting for even a few pennies-worth of drink. So I kept saying yes—yes to short-dated yet complex jobs, yes to scheduling more interviews for my books, yes to pitching as many articles as I had ideas. I was ready, willing, and eager, even when a publisher asked for as-yet unwritten sections of my book. I could handle it, right? This was what I had been waiting for! It was my big chance!

So why was I suddenly so tired that getting out of bed after eight hours of sleep was a struggle? Why did a respiratory infection refuse to go away? Why were my leaps for joy steadily losing altitude?

I decided that I was simply under too much stress and that was why I was drained, physically and psychologically. It made sense, except that this was supposedly good stress. It definitely wasn't bad stress, which comes from bad events such as job loss, health issues, and relationship problems. Shouldn't the good stress that comes from an unexpected promotion, a lottery win, or a new lover fill one with liveliness, power, and *joie de vivre*?

But good stress, like bad stress, is the end product of change, and change, by its very nature, brings elements of the unexpected into our lives. Being creatures of habit, we do our best to keep everything the same, even when change demands a certain amount of alterations. We may want change and we may even pray nightly for it, but at the same time, we like our comfort zone and are determined to hang on to it.

For example, a woman with a new baby may love her new state of motherhood but at the same time is determined to keep her life under control. She tries to work the same hours, keep up with the housework, and even look as fit as she did before her pregnancy. Often the end result is that she is exhausted in mind and body and unable to enjoy the change that she had longed for.

A promotion at work brings more money, more opportunities, and the unsettling feeling that one must immediately get up to speed with the new job responsibilities. An endless round of catch-up ensues, until the newly titled becomes the totally tired who is unable to take pleasure in the advancement.

Even a lottery win can become a bad thing. Research has shown that people who win the lottery have a whole new set of stresses in their lives, from suddenly surfacing relatives seeking handouts to tax problems that are reserved for the rich-and-famous.

To conquer good stress, we have to exercise our adaptability muscle and become more psychologically flexible and more emotionally limber. Let go of the constraints that tell us what we ought to be doing despite the shift in circumstance. Accept the fact that everything—including our own opinion—is now open to review and revision of what we are capable of doing. Here are four guidelines on how to be more adaptable:

1. *Adaptability requires acceptance.* We need to acknowledge that what worked for us before may not work for us now and that we need to alter our order of priorities if we want to reduce stress.

The stress we are experiencing may truly be the result of the change in our lives, or it could be because we aren't willing or able to reorder our priorities to allow for the shifts that have occurred. Is the new mother stressed because she can't keep up with things the way she used to or because she hasn't reordered her priorities to include the demands of motherhood?

Are your priorities all really that critical? Take a pen and paper and make a list of the top five priorities that were in place before the latest change in your life. Now create a second list of your top priorities now, keeping the total number confined to five. (One of those items on the list should be you—

your health and well being.) You'll see immediately that one or more items from the first list had to go to make room for new ones. You may have also had to shift your priority order as well. With the second list, you'll feel more in control and in charge of how your time and energy are spent because you've made a mindful change in your priorities.

2. *Adaptability involves abandonment.* Are we stressed because we can't let go of what had worked for us in the past? We want to hang on to our old schedule or our old routine because it is familiar. Adaptability often requires letting go of the old routine in order to be able to create a new one.

I don't mean that you should give up your twice-weekly workout sessions because you think your job requires it, or not get enough sleep because you want to watch the 11 o'clock news, even though the baby wakes up early. Self-care should never be sacrificed.

David M. Sauvé, personal and business coach and owner of Abundance By Design in British Columbia, said, "It's easy to become mono-focused during transition. [But] a list of some healthy daily habits (not 'to-dos') will smooth out the transition."

Now that you've made your list of priorities, take a hard look at your schedule and see what needs to be changed to keep your priorities in place. Can you schedule your exercise sessions before work, at lunch, or before you go home? Can you watch the early morning news while you feed the baby? Once you admit that everything can't stay the same, you can move on to making a new routine for your new set of circumstances.

3. *Adaptability demands adherence.* We can't just give lip service to our new way of life; we must adhere to the new priorities we have established and the new rules we have made for ourselves. Put your new routine in your datebook or on a calendar, since writing things down often gives them more weight and more importance. Make a commitment to your new plan—and stick to it.

4. *Adaptability necessitates absolution.* Stress often doesn't come from the change itself but from our inability to allow ourselves to be human. We think we should be able to do it all and, like the Energizer Bunny, keep on going. We need to forgive ourselves for not being Superman or Superwoman, for not being able to do everything and be everything to everyone. Of course we really think we should be able to add new responsibilities to our life without giving up any of the old ones. We really like it when people compliment us on how tidy the house is with three kids under age five, or when our boss praises us for an impossibly quick turnaround on a last-minute project. We're only human. The problem is that the people complimenting us rarely know what we had to sacrifice to achieve this remarkable feat.

Despite what advertisements tell us, we can't have it all. Or, as Oprah Winfrey was quoted as saying, "You can have it all. You just can't have it all at once."[1] We aren't bad or incompetent just because we can't do everything. We just have to assign a level of importance to the different aspects of our life and make our decisions based on that reprioritized list.

Life is always in a state of flux. Just when we think we have a plan, life throws us a curve and we have to readjust. It doesn't matter if the change is good or bad. As Sauvé pointed out, "It's all about choices, and change represents choices, opportunities, and challenges."

We may not have a choice about the changes that come into our lives but we do have a choice in how we react to them. It's how we handle change, far more than the change itself, that will determine its effect on our lives.

Part III:
Moving Forward

14

The Pantry of the Soul

My mother kept the equivalent of a pantry in the basement. It was actually a fruit cellar that was colder than the rest of the basement and smelled vaguely of mold and dirt. It wasn't an unpleasant smell but rather like the scent of a garden after a soft rain.

This pantry was filled with canned fruits and vegetables (homemade and store-bought), bottles of soda pop, and bins of potatoes and onions, the result of my mother's goal to keep its shelves well stocked. Even after my brother, sister, and I moved into homes of our own, my mother continued to buy in quantity. Now when I visit my parents' considerably smaller condominium, I find her pantry area still fully laden, a treasure trove of nourishment.

Perhaps that is what most of us need—not necessarily a physical pantry of cans and jars but a spiritual one. Then when we hunger for good thoughts or nourishing emotions, we could go to the shelves and take what we need: the embrace of a lover, the encouraging words of a friend, even the vision of a beautiful summer sunrise, painting the dark sky with gentle bands of rose and gold.

Day Cummings, founder and president of Circle of Daughters Inc., a New York-based organization that serves the bereaved, was only eight years old when her mother passed away. Since then she has drawn on her recollections to give her strength and determination. "It is during the times of sadness, longing, and uncertainty that the memories of her sustain me," she said.

"Infinite riches are all around you if you will open your mental eyes and behold the treasure house of infinity within you," promised Joseph Murphy, PhD, author of *The Power of Your Subconscious Mind*. "There is a gold mine within you from which you can extract everything you need to live life gloriously, joyously and abundantly."[1] But we can't have a stockpile of mental provisions if we don't take the time to shop. We need to spend time each day creating memories from daily events, preserving those precious moments like juicy cherries, dropping them one by one into clear glass jars and then sealing them against the decay of time.

One of my most precious memories is of the second time I saw my daughter, Samantha. The first view came as they were wheeling me out of the delivery room. A nurse held her up for me to see, and all that registered was a shock of dark hair and a red, wrinkled face. She was crying out of fear and pain, and I, seeing a newborn for the first time in my entire life, wondered, where was the beatific smile that figured so prominently on all the baby books I had read during the last nine months?

But then a short time later, they brought her to my room, and when she opened her incredibly large dark eyes to look at me, I fell hopelessly and helplessly in love. My daughter is an adult now with a child of her own, but when I recall that vision of her as a newborn, I feel again that incredibly satisfying maternal emotion.

Other recollections are also stored in my pantry, like the first time I sold an article to a magazine and the editor called to discuss the payment terms. I was so overcome by my success in achieving what had hitherto been nothing more than a dream that I could barely string six words into a coherent sentence. (The man must have hoped that I wrote better than I spoke.) I recall the first time that I signed my name to mortgage papers, not as co-owner with a spouse or with a guarantor but just my name—me, a single woman who had earned enough to be considered financially trustworthy. Now whenever I am contemplating some major financial transaction and doubting my ability to handle it, I pull that memory down from the shelf, carefully unscrew the lid, and take a deep whiff of the fragrance of self-sufficiency. That often enables me to move forward.

But it doesn't have to be a first-time event to be worthy of our pantry shelf. There are quiet moments that nevertheless hold much healing and joy: an autumn evening, with the scent of woodsmoke in the air and the sight of leaves flaming bronze and gold; a dazzling winter morning after the first snowfall, when the world has turned into a fairyland of white; the rhythmic lapping of waves on a beach, lulling you into a sleepy daze.

Author and theologian Tryon Edwards said, "The secret of a good memory is attention, and attention to a subject depends upon our interest in it. We rarely forget that which has made a deep impression on our minds."[2] We must be fully aware of these experiences when they occur, note them as events to be remembered, and keep them easily accessible.

Take a moment and think about times in your life when you felt whole, complete, empowered, and loved. Remember those golden moments when the path you were following was smooth and straight and how the fear that had dogged your footsteps miraculously melted away. Remember the challenges you faced and overcame and the tests you endured and survived. Live them again, wholly and completely, and then take all those feelings and preserve them for a time when you will need the confidence, strength, and security to handle a crisis. Label them and then place the jars safely in your mental pantry, ready for use.

If you'd like, you can also go a step further and preserve those moments in writing. Keep a special journal and record the memories that nourish you. Turn to your journal and reflect on what you have written whenever you need comfort, support, and confidence.

Your pantry can also hold dreams, desires, hopes, and plans. I had an experience several years ago that I believe was a moment of precognition. I was vacuuming the hallway (a mindless task conducive to thinking about other things) and suddenly in the space of a breath I was in the hallway of some multistory office building. I knew, and I don't know how I knew, that it was my publisher's editorial offices. My dear friend Itala was there with me. She wanted me to go shopping with her, but I had to decline. "I have galleys to proof and another book to work on," I explained, and then, just as quickly, I was back in my own hallway again, still vacuuming.

Did I drop out of reality for a moment? Was I lost in a fantasy I had created? For me, the experience was as real as a memory of an actual event. I knew, in that flash of an instant, that someday I would have to decline an afternoon outing because my book needed my attention. I'll never forget that experience, and on occasion, when I doubt if I will be anything more than a freelance writer covering market trends and product sales, I conjure that memory, savor it, and then move back into the real world, resolving to take another step toward that future.

Was there a time when you formulated goals for yourself, personally or professionally, and then set them aside, only to have them forgotten? Dig through the rubble of your recollections, wipe away the cobwebs, and bring those imaginings into the light of day. Place them front and center in your pantry so that every time you open the door, there they are, reminding you of what you want to achieve in your life, showing you what you can be if you try.

One more task needs to be done before your soul's pantry is ready for use. Check each shelf carefully, move boxes and bottles, and look in the corners and behind the jars. You may have overlooked some "spoiled" items: containers of spiritual food that will make you ill instead of nourish you or leave the taste of bitterness in your heart. Have you inadvertently brought into your pantry those negative items whose very presence can contaminate the healthy ones?

There, behind the jar of your first embrace—are those the harsh words from a failed love affair? Under the box of professional success—could that be a carton of negative feedback from someone close to you? Discard these items in the largest trash container you can find. Don't hold on to times of failure and pain unless you are able to find the silver thread in them—the lesson they taught you or the strength they engendered. If they smell only of disappointment, deceit, sorrow, or weakness, discard them. They have no place in your pantry.

When we begin to stock our pantry, we must search out the best provisions to place on the shelves. And as we sniff, touch, and taste each occurrence—when we pay closer attention to hugs from a friend and kisses from our child—we realize what a wealth of nourishment can be drawn from these experiences not only when they occur but also when they are remembered. Our pantry of the soul becomes a place filled with golden moments of happiness found in everyday life from which we can draw sustenance and encouragement.

15

The Hidden Advantage of Hindrances

Have you ever noticed that sometimes the path ahead is smooth and easy to navigate, while other times it is strewn with roadblocks? While change may result when we overcome obstacles, other times it may occur when we are prevented from reaching our intended destination.

I had been in a relationship for seven years, with marriage as the unstated outcome. During what turned out to be our last year together, my partner and I began house-hunting. It was an ill-fated venture that covered two states and five counties. Real estate agents failed to keep appointments or lacked the information we needed. Houses that would be perfect for our needs faced noisy manufacturing facilities, backed onto busy highways, or were next door to eyesores. Lovely pieces of property, some even complete with running streams or babbling brooks, were also the site of residences that only a cockeyed optimist would call a "fixer-upper."

Sunday after Sunday we attended open houses, and hour after hour we perused real estate ads. Entire conversations were devoted to the relative merits of gas versus electric heat or vinyl siding versus brick. Tellingly enough, none of our conversations dealt with our life together—they all dealt with finding the perfect house.

Near the end of our last summer together, I called my mother and complained about yet another disappointing venture. "If it didn't work out, then there's a good reason," she said, in an effort to be consoling. "It just wasn't meant to be."

As it turned out, she was right. Not too long after that call, I ended the relationship. Something was lacking that didn't have anything to do with where we were going to live; it was more about how we would live together and how we would be able to reconcile our two very different attitudes and priorities. I knew that our differences were so great that no house would be big enough to contain them.

If any of the houses had been "the one," if any of our offers had been accepted or if the deals had gone through, we would have been married and living unhappily ever after. There were so many roadblocks and none of our house-hunting trips were met with success because the relationship "wasn't meant to be." If I hadn't had my eyes so firmly focused on finding a house, if I had stopped looking long enough to see what was so plainly before me, I could have saved us both a lot of time and heartache.

I have since come to realize that sometimes roadblocks are put in our life to challenge us, make us grow, and give us a sense of accomplishment after we overcome them, but sometimes they are there to slow us down, give us time to reflect, and keep us from rushing headlong over the cliff to certain disaster. The trick is to distinguish between these two reasons.

If every hurdle we cross leads to a higher one, if every time we solve a problem, another one surfaces, maybe we need to look at where we're heading to make sure that the destination is worth the effort. Maybe we are so focused on winning the battle that we haven't analyzed if this is a war we should even be involved in. Maybe we are so intent on winning the prize that we haven't asked ourselves if it is even a prize we want any longer. Or maybe we are just too stubborn to consider another alternative; maybe we keep pushing forward because it's what we've always done and there is a certain security in staying on track.

In the children's movie *Labyrinth*, a young girl named Sarah desperately tries to find her way through a stone-walled maze. She rushes up and down the narrow pathway, unable to find a way that will take her to the center. It isn't until she stops from exhaustion that a small creature is able to catch her attention and point out the very opening she had been searching for. It had been there all along but not where she thought it would be and wouldn't have been visible if she hadn't stopped moving.

If the road we are moving along is leading us nowhere, if the obstacles increase instead of decrease, and if we are more tired than energized by the struggle, maybe it's time we stopped long enough to listen for that small quiet voice that can point out a different way to travel.

As Elisabeth Kübler-Ross pointed out in *Death Is of Vital Importance*, "It took me fifty years to realize that . . . the things we regard as tragedies are not really tragedies unless we choose to make tragedies out of them. Because we can also choose to regard them as chances for us, opportunities to grow, and then we see that they are challenges and hints that we may need to change our lives."[1]

But how do we determine if we should continue to push ahead or change our course entirely? What is the difference between being a quitter or being someone wise enough to know when to move on? Simply put, when is enough *enough*?

If you are facing this situation, it might be helpful to ask yourself the following questions:

1. *Do you find yourself envisioning a successful outcome or fantasizing about other alternatives?*

The biggest source of encouragement should be found in your own mind and in the future you are creating with your own imagination. You should be able to envision success even when dealing with problems. But if your mind is filled with an imagined future that is dramatically different from the one you are working toward, perhaps you need to rethink your path.

My friend Betsy spent years as a flight attendant, and for a long time she found the lifestyle acceptable and at times quite satisfying. But as she entered her thirties, her body began to rebel against the long hours and lack of downtime, and her mind stopped dreaming of the next advancement and instead turned toward being at home and spending time with friends and family. Eventually she realized that all the obstacles that were part of career advancement were no longer appropriate for her, and she chose to leave that life and explore other options.

2. *Are your priorities and life goals the same as when you started this course or have they changed significantly?*

Perhaps you decided long ago that being an executive was your life ambition. You spent years climbing the corporate ladder, enlivened by the challenges. Then you got married, had a baby, were faced with a life-threatening decision, or woke up one day and wondered what else you could be.

The term "midlife crisis" is often used to define major changes people make as they reach their late thirties and early forties. Unfortunately the phrase has acquired negative connotations: the fortysomething woman who has face-lift after face-lift, or the fortysomething man who leaves his family for a much-younger woman. I prefer the term "priority shift," since so often the change occurs as a result of a shift in our values. What we had once thought was important may no longer be, and what we had once considered a mark of success may no longer matter. This doesn't mean that the standards and goals we had had in the past were wrong. They may have been right for the people we were at the time but are no longer appropriate for who we have become. People change, so why shouldn't their dreams, goals, and priorities change as well?

3. *Are you exhausted or energized by the struggle?*

Do you feel worn out or beaten down, as though you are bearing the weight of the world on your shoulders? Do you awaken each morning dreading the path you've chosen? Or do you keep going even when the rest of the world has shut down?

In her autobiography, Agatha Christie recounted how she had written *Absent in the Spring* in only three days, unwilling to resist the creative impulse that drove her. She said, "I don't think I have ever been so tired ... but to have that fatigue and exhaustion was worthwhile."[2] She experienced what Mihaly Csikszentmihalyi calls the "flow," or "being completely involved in an activity for its own sake."[3]

If the path you are on is the right one for you, it will nourish, energize, and beckon you. But if it drains you, pay heed to the hindrance of exhaustion. It's telling you to turn around, go back, and rethink your destination or reroute your trip.

It's not that Road A is filled with problems while Road B is free and clear. Both pathways will have their share of difficulties and impediments. The key is to know when we are ultimately on the right path and able to move forward or when it's time for us to change direction and follow a new course.

16

Letting Go of Illusions

"I'll take a vacation when work eases up." "I'll go back to school when the kids graduate." "I'll change jobs when something better is available."

We've all made promises like these to ourselves, tying a goal to an unrelated circumstance. By taking this approach to life we perpetuate the illusion of moving forward when we really aren't moving at all. And the very real possibility exists that, if and when the circumstances do change, we will be able to come up with new reasons for why we can't take the next step toward achieving our goal.

For example, over the past winter I have gained some weight—not a lot, but just enough and in just the right (or wrong) places to make most of my jeans noticeably tighter. I knew I had to do something about it, and I didn't want to buy new clothes a size larger. My plan was to exercise and eat better, but it was close to the holidays; dieting didn't seem practical. And the cold wind that whistled around the corners of the house blew me right back indoors. I'll work out when it's springtime, I told myself, after the holidays, my birthday, and Easter candy.

Then came a rainy March, followed by an even rainier April, which provided more reasons not to exercise and more justification for drowning my self-disappointment in ice cream. As I enjoyed Rocky Road or Chocolate Chunk, I rationalized my decision by promising that I would work out as soon as the weather warmed up.

Finally the weather did improve and I pulled out my summer shorts in preparation for a heart-pumping walk, only to discover that the zipper wouldn't zip and the button wouldn't button. I had not only not lost weight but I had gained even more by sitting there waiting for "the right time."

If I had stuck to my original plan, I would have traveled my path regardless of the existing circumstances. Instead, I let external conditions dictate how and when I would achieve my goal. As Andy Warhol once said, "They always say that time changes things, but you actually have to change them yourself."[1]

We also need to determine if we have the abilities needed to achieve the goal we've identified and if we are prepared for all the work required to attain it. Otherwise, it's not a true goal but a fantasy that diverts our focus from our current, less palatable life.

Some of us focus on "future fantasies." We picture a life very different from our current one and imagine how much happier we would be in it. Someone I am close to had talked for months about what she envisioned as "the joys of self-employment." She told me how much she hated corporate life, how she dreamed of the day when she could be in charge of her own destiny, and how much better business would run if she had the chance to direct the action. As if to prove the old saying "Be careful what you wish for. You may get it" and as luck, or Fate, would have it, the company she worked for closed down, and she found herself out of work at forty. It gave her the perfect opportunity, one might think, to put her plans into action. But the reality of self-employment—the long hours, the lack of a guaranteed income, the higher percentage of rejections over acceptances— was more than my friend could handle. In the end, she sought to return to the ranks of the employed, unfortunately from a substantially weaker financial position.

My friend learned some valuable lessons about herself, such as where her abilities and personality best fit, when she had a chance to explore her fantasy. But many of us don't have that chance. We live instead in "future fantasies." We don't stop to analyze whether our personality fits our fantasy life, or how we could start incorporating some elements of that dream into our present existence. That would be too realistic and too threatening. Instead, we continue to live in a fantasy world.

Some of us focus on "past fantasies" and how much better our current life would be if we had said or done something in our past, if we had taken the second job offer instead of the first, married Mr. X instead of Mr. Y, had more children or fewer or none at all, or moved across the country instead of choosing to live in our hometown. But we will never really know whether our life would have been substantially different. Certainly some key elements may change, but we, the central component, would remain the same. We would still be the driving force that directs the action and the factor that all other events depend upon. We would have the same personality, the same characteristics, and the same approach to life. Allowing regret to color your life is, as writer Katherine Mansfield put it, "an appalling waste of energy; you can't build on it, it's only good for wallowing in."[2]

On more than one occasion, a woman I know has bemoaned her loveless marriage. She says that her husband, while not a bad man, simply doesn't answer her needs and that she would have left him long ago if she had been able to go to school and support herself. But when others point out her options—that even at her age, divorce is possible and the division of their marital assets would not necessarily place her on public assistance—she changes the subject. She doesn't want to hear reality. She would rather live in a fantasy constructed of regret than look within herself to find what she is willing to surrender to gain what she claims she has longed for during most of her adult life.

There are those who act to remedy the results of past decisions. Although as a child, author Kelly James-Enger had dreamed of being a writer, she chose to pursue a law degree because, as she put it, "I wanted to have a career where I could support myself, and I didn't think I could make a living as a writer. It was easier to keep that in the back of my head as a fantasy than to investigate the steps necessary to make it a reality."

But after practicing law for more than five years, the dream of writing returned, bringing with it fears about her ability to make a living. James-Enger noted, "One of the things that helped me overcome my resistance was to educate myself about freelancing and how the publishing world works; as I learned more about the business and began getting published, I started to believe that I did have a shot of making a go of it full-time."

She put her plan into action, saving enough to cover her expenses for the first six months before quitting to write full-time. "That was more than seven years ago," she said. "Since then, I've written for more than fifty national magazines, have sold five books (two novels, three nonfiction), and have cracked the six-figure mark as a freelancer."

James-Enger's story is an example of how we can't change our reality until we face it. We can't gain control of our life until we begin to live within it again, instead of in our dream world.

We can never know what our life would be like if we had decided to do this instead of that or if we had gone down the road not taken instead of the one we ultimately chose. Spending every waking moment living in the future without taking the steps to bring that future closer is simply building castles in the air.

If you are unhappy with the circumstances of your reality, you must first acknowledge it and make necessary adjustments within your own life. Take some time to objectively evaluate your dream. Are you willing to do what it takes to accomplish it and to deal with its aftermath? Come up with a plan of action. Let go of your illusions and start moving forward into a more fulfilled existence. As author Louise L. Hay wrote, "Remember that this is a new day, and the point of power is always in the present moment."[3]

17

The Danger of "Excessive Obligations"

A few years ago, my credit card application was rejected, not because I had a history of bad credit but because I had what was nicely termed "excessive obligations." In plain English, it meant that I had too much debt. I had taken on more financial burdens than I could reasonably expect to handle.

I was disappointed and chagrined. It was the first time that this had happened in all my years of adulthood. But at the same time, some small part of me was relieved. The decision was made by an outside entity to save me from further financial obligations. Someone had looked out for me and stopped me from getting in over my head. The more I thought about it, the more I realized that perhaps we all need in life some impartial evaluating agency that would weigh the decisions we are planning to make and let us know whether doing so would result in some form of overextension.

For instance, suppose we plan to take on a difficult career assignment when we are already responsible for our home and our children. While we would find the work rewarding, we could also find ourselves working extremely long hours. In this case, we would be running the risk of overextending ourselves and bankrupting our health savings account. If we could present this option to the evaluating agency, it could alert us to dangers that we hadn't foreseen. Its decision would then be binding, until a time when our resources account was greater or our other obligations were less.

Unreasonable expectations put us into a state of "excessive obligation" in which we are not only unable to handle our new "debt" but we also have insufficient resources to pay those that we had previously undertaken. To avoid this we must assume the role of the impartial evaluating agency and ask ourselves some hard questions and take the time to evaluate the extent of our pre-existing obligations before we dive into a situation that could result in physical, mental, or emotional bankruptcy.

1. *Is the interest rate too high?*

Negative reasons are the equivalent of a high finance charge. Every payment we make comes with a high interest rate that results in a debt that takes longer to pay off than we had anticipated. Like interest, negative emotion brings a larger cost and burden to the original investment.

2. *Are our expectations for being able to meet this debt based on a fantasy?*

We tell ourselves that we can handle this new task because so-and-so had promised to help out whenever needed. We believe that promise, even though past events have clearly demonstrated that help probably won't be coming. We assume the new obligation based on the expectation of additional support, but the helpful payments never materialize and we are left with the bill.

3. *Is this debt really ours to assume?*

I had a friend who always borrowed my car. Hers was broken and she said she didn't have the money to fix it. Once or twice would have been fine, but it became a regular, almost expected arrangement. When I finally realized that my car was spending more time in her driveway than in mine, I rethought my decision. It wasn't that I didn't want to help her or that she was a bad person but she had incurred a debt (a car that she couldn't afford to fix) and expected me to help her pay the bill (by loaning her mine). Once I stopped the loan, she found the money to fix her own vehicle and the maturity to realize that her problems were hers to resolve.

4. *Do we have prior debts that should take precedence?*

We spend hours each week working with a local charity when our own family needs our help. We rush to answer a stranger's call for assistance but are never available for our friends. We work long draining hours because we are committed to our career even though we are damaging our own health in the process. Our busy-ness ultimately results in more debt rather than less, because we are, in effect, robbing Peter to pay Paul.

My friend Cindy admits that this is an issue for her. "I get swept up by great ideas and the desire to help and find myself unable to complete everything I've committed to. I have two solutions. First I reduce my expectations for myself. I'm a perfectionist, and I forget that everything doesn't have to be just so. When I stop to reevaluate, I often find that I can do part of what I had intended and achieve what I'd hoped without driving myself crazy or taking as much time. Second, if I still have too much to do, I review my priorities to see which tasks are most important to me.

"Over time," she said, "I've become better at admitting my limits to myself and to others; I don't sign on to everything that comes my way. I leave time for myself to recharge, and when I fail or don't meet my personal expectations I don't beat myself up about it—at least, not as much as I used to."

5. *Are we taking on new obligations to avoid handling the ones we already have?*

If we have an unhappy home life, chances are that instead of resolving the problem at hand, we accept new responsibilities that will take us outside of the house. Our rationale is that if we can't solve the original problem, we'll ignore it and find a new one we can solve. And it works, as writer, speaker, and simplicity guru Elaine St. James succinctly wrote in *Fast Company*: "Maintaining a complicated life is a great way to avoid changing it."[1] Unfortunately the original debt still stands, growing larger as the interest charges accrue.

    6. *Are we looking for applause and accolades?*

We want people to point at us and say, "She is a veritable Wonder Woman! Look how much she does!" But when we assume this debt, we can't expect such a profit.

In addition to asking ourselves these questions, we also have to complete some financial documents for our life, including a balance sheet and a profit-and-loss statement. The balance sheet will reflect our assets (what strengths we have) and our liabilities (what long-term obligations we have already contracted for). The profit-and-loss statement reflects the income and outflow of resources that allow us to function on a daily basis. If we have regular expenses we need to meet, such as daily child-care duties or volunteer work, then we can't assume new bills without increasing our income. We may need to ask other people to provide more assistance or cancel one bill in favor of another.

If, for example, a parent requires extensive care due to a health problem, we may be able to shift some of the other expenses we've been responsible for to our partner's side of the books. If we want to return to school in order to advance in our career or change it completely, we may be able to ask our children to take on more responsibility around the home. If we want to support a new cause, we may have to cut back on the time we spend with other charities.

Essentially we are following a sound business strategy for running the business of our life. We are taking a proactive approach and planning for change, instead of simply making the change and then dealing with the aftermath. We may find, after careful thought and consideration, that the obligation we would like to assume should wait until circumstances are more favorable.

We might also learn that the assistance we had thought would be forthcoming simply won't be available, which tells us something about the reasonableness of our expectations. Perhaps the relationship is not as supportive as we had once believed. Or perhaps the other person is struggling with his or her own debts and is simply not able to help us at this time. This doesn't make the other person selfish or incompetent. After all, we must allow others to use the same method as we do when making their choices. Their answer adds to our knowledge base and tells us what we can reasonably expect to receive in the future.

Once we have analyzed our expectations, we will be in a better place to decide what, if anything, we need to do. And if we choose to assume the new obligation, our decision will come out of a better place and be driven by healthier emotions. We won't feel resentful or imposed upon.

Whatever our decision may be, if made for the right reasons, it can result in a lightness of the heart and an energizing boost to the spirit. A friend of mine had been involved in a family relationship that her friends could see was detrimental to her health and happiness. She spent all her time trying to make it work, when it was clearly apparent that the other party wasn't interested in making any changes. In the meantime, my friend began to suffer from abdominal problems, migraines, and insomnia that resulted in a long and expensive round of medical tests to find the cause. Instead of enjoying life, she spent her days in a state of depression.

Finally she gave her relative the gift of limits, setting a boundary between them that removed her from the land of victimization and put her back into the country of control. Once the crisis passed, my friend's health problems began to disappear and her energy level returned to normal. She could move forward with her own life because she eliminated the debt she had contracted. Problems that before seemed insurmountable now could be resolved. The future suddenly seemed open to possibilities. My friend was experiencing what inspirational writer Catherine Ponder said would happen: "It's amazing how fast doors open to us when we dare to take control of a situation."[2]

I suppose that one day I will reapply for that same credit card and be given the green light. But this will happen only if I spend the time now to take a hard look at what my debts are, develop a plan to reduce them, and then put that plan into action. And the same applies for those times when I feel overwhelmed by emotional burdens. I'll need to evaluate what debts are mine to assume and work at eliminating those that belong in someone else's books. Only then will I have the necessary resources to move forward.

18

Planting a Garden

I am on a planting kick. I dig the hard-as-concrete clay soil out back to create a narrow rectangular garden and then excavate a flower bed at the opposite end of my property. Not content with the results of my labor and undeterred by the blisters on my palms, I move a maple sapling from the place where it was perfectly comfortable to another area entirely and create an island around it, which will, if this trend continues, become longer and wider as the summer goes on.

When I'm not digging, I'm spreading mulch. Bag by bag, cubic foot by cubic foot, I pour and apply, covering the dry earth with a blanket of moisture-retaining tree bark. When I run out of mulch, each trip to the store has me reciting the same lines: "I just need two more bags of mulch. That's all. And then I'm done."

But the two bags are never enough, and so I get two more and then two more again. There's always more bare earth than mulch and there's always another area that could benefit from the protection it offers. Even as I write, I see the light-colored dirt peeking through the darker blanket of tree shreds and wonder if two more bags would do the trick or if four more cubic feet would be enough.

For me, playing in the dirt, which is what my gardening really is, since it is too small to be truly considered work, has always been supremely satisfying. As a child, I spent hours in the neighbor's sandbox, excavating roads and building mountains, creating a world from grains of sand. I was powerful. I could make entire towns out of nothing but dirt and my own exertions. It was my first experience with the creative process, my first awareness that I could make a world solely from my own efforts.

Digging a garden or constructing a flower bed offers the same benefit to me now. I sow seeds and set out starter plants, and, in the process, create an existence rooted in the present but producing in the future. Like God, I am giving life an opportunity to grow, but, unlike God, I, too, am changed in the process.

Planting a garden exposes my own vulnerability and allows my own fears to flourish. Will the birds pick the seeds

from the soil before they have a chance to sprout? Will the sun-
light dry out the tender leaves or will the rainfall drown the
thread-like roots? Will the weeds choke the young plants or
will the rabbits nibble away at the stems until there is nothing
left? Each day, I measure the growth of my plants and marvel
that, against all odds, they are continuing to develop.

And while I am out there tilling the soil and planting the
seeds, I am thinking. I burrow through the topsoil in my mind
and find, as in my real-world garden, that sometimes the
ground gives way and other times it resists the turning and
cultivating process. There are emotions deeply rooted that, if
left alone, will grow like weeds. There are others that hold the
promise of flowering if I can keep the environment around
them healthy and rich.

I discover memories that I had carefully avoided, not want-
ing to admit failures or relive the pain, but I keep digging and
hoeing, shoving the spade in a little deeper each time. By turning over those recollections buried deeply in my mind, I can
expose them to the healing sunshine and nurturing rain. Each
day, I cultivate a little more of my inner garden, hoping to make
it a more nourishing place for new thoughts and feelings to grow.

Of course, as any gardener will tell you, the tilling and
planting process is only the beginning. Between the hope of
seeds germinating and the enjoyment of fruits and vegetables
lies a long hot summer of weeding, watering, and feeding.

Weeds have a way of taking root anywhere, most particularly where you don't want them. Every morning finds me on my hands and knees, pulling out unwanted visitors that have grown overnight, like Jack's beanstalk, to amazing heights. No matter how many I pull, more will surface the next morning. It's a never-ending process.

Negative thoughts, like weeds, come up everywhere, twisting their tendrils around our lives and, if not summarily removed, choking the life from them. It's a constant battle that requires the utmost vigilance: We must be on the lookout for attitudes that grow from pessimism, anger, and disappointment and dig deep to remove them, roots and all. With time and effort, it is possible that eventually the seeds these thoughts spring from will grow fewer in number, until the healthy plants—love, peace, faith, and serenity—outnumber them.

A healthy garden also requires nourishment—food and drink to give it the strength to go through the long hot summer. I once returned from a three-day trip to find my bean plants nearly lifeless. I drenched the soil with water, and by evening the plants had perked up a bit, deciding to forgive me for my neglect. Days later I found blossoms on the stems and eventually experienced the satisfaction of pulling slender green beans from the curling tendrils. I have an unspoken contract with my garden: I will give it what it requires and it, in turn, will provide vegetables in abundance.

We, too, require nourishment, the life force that makes us stronger, healthier, and more likely to produce. Life may be a work in progress, but that doesn't necessarily mean that it should be hard, unpleasant, and unsatisfying. If we want to produce, we must feed our minds and souls—and the "food" we need is all around us. Watching the night darkness as it gives way to a palette of colors streaking across the sky, hearing the music of a child's laugh, feeling the touch of a lover's hand—these soul-feeding moments provide the sustenance that allows us to continue living.

We owe it to ourselves and to the others who will benefit from our life garden to do all that we can to encourage our own growth. We must extract as much nourishment as possible from everyday events and spend at least as much time experiencing life as working on it. Gardening is hard work. So is life. But it can be immensely satisfying if we pay attention to the process every step of the way. We must taste, touch, smell, listen, and, most importantly, acknowledge what we see and feel.

We all need a garden or, at the very least, a plant or two in a windowsill pot. We need to experience the life-giving force by watching a seed, apparently dry and lifeless, sprout with vigor, measuring the growth of a delicate stem, and observing a swelling become a bud and then a fragrant flower.

May Sarton wrote in *Journal of a Solitude* that, for her, flowers are felt as presences. "They change before my eyes.

They live and die in a few days; they keep me closely in touch with the process, with growth and also with dying."[1] The ever-present cycle of life—growth, fruition, and death—keeps us grounded in the real world and also fills us with hope.

Especially during the darkest times of our lives, we need to remind ourselves that growth is always present and always an option, that seeds won't germinate and plants won't root if the soil that surrounds them is hard, packed, and dry, that the life-giving force is always available to us if we just dig far enough and deep enough, that seemingly soul-destroying events can be experiences that allow us to grow, expand, and develop.

And this growth has a double benefit. Not only does it improve our own life but it also allows us to share this largesse with others around us. Like a tree that has progressed from a twelve-inch sapling to a sturdy sixty-foot maple, we can shade someone who lives in an emotional desert with companionship. Like the flowering rosebush laden with blossoms, we can offer the grieving the delicate fragrance of sympathy. And like the twisted branches of the grapevine, heavily laden with thirst-quenching purple globes, we can provide the nourishment of life to one starving for want of affection.

Gardening is a never-ending process, a series of changes that begins with the planting of a single seed and continues on until the harvest. Throughout the entire growing season, changes take place in the soil and weather conditions as well as in the plant itself. These changes are necessary to bring the plant to fruition and to ultimately provide us with flowers, fruits, and vegetables—nourishment for all the senses.

Changes occur in our lives as well, and if we are open to them and use them fully, they can generate internal growth that will bring us to full flowering. And that is the gift of change.

Notes

Chapter 1

1. "Inspiration a Day," Motivational Quotes.com, http://www.motivationalquotes.com.

2. Arlene F. Benedict, *Believing in Ourselves: The Journey Ahead* (Kansas City, MO: Andrews McMeel Publishing, 1997), 12.

Chapter 2

1. Writer's Digest, "Eleven Tips for Priming Your Creativity," *Writer's Digest*, http://www.writersdigest.com/articles/newsletter/fuel_creativity.asp?secondarycategory=Fiction+Subhome+Page.

2. Quote DB—The Quotations Database, http://www.quotedb.com/quotes/12.

3. To Inspire.com, http://www.toinspire.com.

Chapter 3

1. Mihaly Csikszentmihalyi, *Creativity: Flow and the Psychology of Discovery and Invention* (New York: HarperCollins, 1996), quoted in Motivational Quotes.com, http://www.sperience.org/jpages/education-quotes.html.

2. Thomas Crum, *Journey to Center* (New York: Fireside, 1997), 39.

Chapter 4

1. Lawrence LeShan, *Meditating to Attain a Healthy Body Weight* (New York: Doubleday, 1994), quoted in Myfit.ca, http://www.myfit.ca/news/news_comments.asp?NewsID=46.

2. Jean Shinoda Bolen, "Windows of the Soul," in *Handbook for the Soul*, edited by Richard Carlson and Benjamin Shield. (New York: Little, Brown, 1995), 7.

Chapter 5

1. Greg Anderson, *The 22 Non-Negotiable Laws of Wellness* (San Francisco: HarperSanFrancisco, 1996), quoted in Sundberg-Ferar's Web site, "About Us, Offices," http://www.shapetomorrow.com/aboutus/offices.html.

2. Crum, 168–9 (see chap. 3, n. 2).

3. Meredith Young-Sowers, *Angelic Messenger Cards for Divine Guidance* (Walpole, NH: Stillpoint Publishing, 1993).

4. Crum, 168–9.

5. Melody Beattie, *The Language of Letting Go* (Center City, MN: Hazelden Information Education, 1996), 71–72.

Chapter 6

1. Wayne Muller, *Sabbath: Remembering the Sacred Rhythm of Rest and Delight* (New York: Bantam Books, 1999), quoted in *Paauwerfully Organized*, April 2001, http://www.orgcoach.net/newsletter/april2001.html.

2. Lillian Eichler Watson, ed., *Light from Many Lamps* (New York: Simon & Schuster, 1951), 49–50.

3. Joan Z. Borysenko, *Inner Peace for Busy Women* (Carlsbad, CA: Hay House, 2003), 96.

Chapter 7

1. Dennis Wholey, *The Miracle of Change* (New York: Pocket Books, 1997), 63.

2. Crum, 64 (see chap. 3, n. 2).

3. Anne Wilson Schaef, *Meditations for Women Who Do Too Much* (New York: HarperCollins, 1990), Sept. 10.

4. The Learning Center Newsletter, December 2002, http://www.learningassistance.com/2002/Dec02/quotes.htm.

5. Aphorisms Galore! http://www.ag.wastholm.net/aphorism/A-1139.

Chapter 8

1. Robert Fulghum, *All I Really Need to Know I Learned in Kindergarten: Uncommon Thoughts on Common Things* (New York: Villard Books, 1986), 6–7.

2. Barbara Sher, *I Could Do Anything If I Only Knew What It Was* (New York: DTP, 1995), 98.

3. Susan Shaughnessy, *Walking on Alligators: A Book of Meditations for Writers* (San Francisco: HarperSanFrancisco, 1993), 10.

Chapter 9

1. Susan Jeffers, *Feel the Fear and Do It Anyway*, rev. ed (New York: Balantine Books, 1987), 15.

2. Ibid., 30.

Chapter 10

1. Peter McWilliams, *You Can't Afford the Luxury of a Negative Thought* (Santa Monica: Prelude Press, 1997), quoted in Peter McWilliams's Web site, http://www.mcwilliams.com/books/books/lux/lx1a.htm.

Chapter 11

1. Sarah Ban Breathnach, *Simple Abundance: A Daybook of Comfort and Joy* (New York: Warner Books, 1995), March 1.

2. BrainyQuote, http://www.brainyquote.com/quotes/quotes/m/mihalycsik130820.html.

Chapter 12

1. BrainyQuote, http://www.brainyquote.com/quotes/quotes/c/charlesdic138512.html.

2. Neale Donald Walsch, "What I Know for Sure," *O: The Oprah Magazine*, April 2001, 232.

3. Young-Sowers (see chap. 5, n. 3).

Chapter 13

1. Quote DB—The Quotations Database, http://www.quotedb.com/quotes/1721.

Chapter 14

1. Joseph Murphy, *The Power of Your Subconscious Mind*, rev. ed. (New York: Bantam, 2001), quoted in "The Golden Storehouse of the Subconscious Mind," http://www.angelfire.com/journal/fridaysinspiration/archives/111700.html.

2. The Quotations Page, http://www.quotationspage.com/quotes.php3?author=Tryon+Edwards.

Chapter 15

1. Elisabeth Kübler-Ross, *Death Is Of Vital Importance* (Barrytown, NY: Station Hill Press, 1995), 1.

2. *Agatha Christie, An Autobiography* (New York: Balantine Books, 1977), 603.

3. Mihaly Csikszentmihalyi, *Flow: The Psychology of Optimal Experience* (New York: HarperCollins, 1991), quoted in Yale University Digital Media Center for the Arts's Web site, http://www.dmca.yale.edu/interactiveartspace/flow.html.

Chapter 16

1. Music Thoughts, http://www.musicthoughts.com/t/619.

2. "Regrets," http://www.angelfire.com/ky/sarahfina/regrets.html.

3. Louise L. Hay, *Empowering Women: Every Woman's Guide to Successful Living* (Carlsbad, CA: Hay House, 1997), 53.

Chapter 17

1. Elaine St. James, "6 Ways to Simplify Your Life," *Fast Company*, June 1998, 154.

2. Benedict, 22 (see chap. 1, n. 2).

Chapter 18

1. May Sarton, *Journal of a Solitude* (New York: W. W. Norton, 1973), 11.

Resource List/Suggested Reading

Anderson, Greg. *The 22 Non-Negotiable Laws of Wellness.* San Francisco: HarperSanFrancisco, 1996.

Beattie, Melody. *The Language of Letting Go.* Center City, MN: Hazelden Information Education, 1996.

Borysenko, Joan Z. *Inner Peace for Busy Women.* Carlsbad, CA: Hay House, 2003.

Breathnach, Sarah Ban. *Simple Abundance: A Daybook of Comfort and Joy.* New York: Warner Books, 1995.

Christie, Agatha. *Agatha Christie, An Autobiography.* New York: Balantine Books, 1977.

Crum, Thomas. *Journey to Center.* New York: Fireside, 1997.

Ditzler, Jinny S. *Your Best Year Yet!* New York: Warner Books, 2000.

Dyer, Wayne W. *The Power of Intention: Learning to Co-Create Your World Your Way.* Carlsbad, CA: Hay House, 2004.

Frankl, Viktor E. *Man's Search For Meaning.* Rev. ed. New York: Pocket Books, 1997.

Hay, Louise L. *Empowering Women: Every Woman's Guide to Successful Living.* Carlsbad, CA: Hay House, 1997.

Heilbrun, Carolyn G. *Writing a Woman's Life.* Rev. ed. New York: Ballantine Books, 1989.

Jeffers, Susan, PhD. *Embracing Uncertainty: Breakthrough Methods for Achieving Peace of Mind When Facing the Unknown.* New York: St. Martin's Press, 2003.

————. *Feel The Fear and Do It Anyway.* Rev. ed. New York: Balantine Books, 1987.

Katselas, Milton. *Dreams Into Action: Getting What You Want.* Beverly Hills, CA: Katselas Productions, 1996.

Klauser, Henriette Anne. *Write It Down, Make It Happen.* New York: Simon & Schuster, 2001.

Peck, M. Scott. *The Road Less Traveled.* New York: Touchstone Books, 2003.

Pederson, Rena. *What's Missing?: Inspiration for Women Seeking Faith and Joy in Their Lives.* New York: Perigee, 2003.

————. *What's Next?: Women Redefining Their Dreams in the Prime of Life.* With Dr. Lee Smith. New York: Perigee, 2001.

Schaef, Anne Wilson, PhD. *Meditations for Women Who Do Too Much.* New York: HarperCollins, 1990.

Seligman, Martin. *Learned Optimism: How to Change Your Mind and Your Life.* Rev. ed. New York: Free Press, 1998.

Sher, Barbara. *I Could Do Anything If I Only Knew What It Was.* New York,: DTP, 1995.

Sills, Judith, PhD. *Excess Baggage: Getting Out of Your Own Way.* Rev. ed. New York: Penguin USA, 1994.

Sinetar, Marsha. *To Build the Life You Want, Create the Work You Love.* New York: St. Martin's Press, 1995.

Thoele, Sue Patton. *Growing Hope: Sowing the Seeds of Positive Change in Your Life and the World.* Berkeley, CA: Conari Press, 2004.

————. *The Woman's Book of Soul.* New York: M J F Books, 2000.

Watson, Lillian Eichler, ed. *Light from Many Lamps.* New York: Simon & Schuster, 1951.

Wholey, Dennis. *The Miracle of Change.* New York: Pocket Books, 1997.

Young-Sowers, Meredith. *Angelic Messenger Cards for Divine Guidance.* Walpole, NH: Stillpoint Publishing, 1993.

Every day, you have the opportunity to stretch your boundaries, explore untapped areas of potential and discover hidden talents. But making a change, even a small one, can be a little unnerving, requiring us, as Thoreau said, "to leap in the dark to our success."

To help you on your journey of change, I've created a "Make a Change" page on my *www.giftsofchange.com* web site. Each month, there will be new suggestions to help you expand your sense of possibility. Try one, try all -success lies in making the journey, not in reaching the destination.

Beyond Words Publishing, Inc.

OUR CORPORATE MISSION

Inspire to Integrity

OUR DECLARED VALUES

We give to all of life as life has given us.
We honor all relationships.
Trust and stewardship are integral to fulfilling dreams.
Collaboration is essential to create miracles.
Creativity and aesthetics nourish the soul.
Unlimited thinking is fundamental.
Living your passion is vital.
Joy and humor open our hearts to growth.
It is important to remind ourselves of love.

To order or to request a catalog, contact
Beyond Words Publishing, Inc.
20827 N.W. Cornell Road, Suite 500
Hillsboro, OR 97124-9808
503-531-8700

You can also visit our Web site at *www.beyondword.com*.

Printed in the United States
By Bookmasters